D1075083

DISCARDED
WIDENER UNIVERSITY

JAMES STEPHENS

JAMES STEPHENS

His Work and an Account of His Life

by

HILARY PYLE

NEW YORK
BARNES & NOBLE, INC.

*First published
in the United States of America
1965
© Hilary Pyle* 1965

WIDENER UNIVERSITY
WOLFGRAM
LIBRARY
CHESTER, PA.

PR
6037
.T4
Z83

20th C SHORT STORY EXPL.

Printed in Great Britain

TO HUG

Contents

Plates

Preface

TO attempt a biography of James Stephens may be a matter for question. It is well known that he deplored the modern tendency to dwell on the sensational elements in an author's life to the neglect of what is most important, his writing, and the similar tendency to disregard altogether what the man has written. He stated definitely on more than one occasion that a writer's life bears no relation to his work. But it is an opinion which leaves room for debate, and his sensitivity on this point may have lingered from his early days when he was launched into a world totally different, both socially and intellectually, from that in which he had been reared, where his curious appearance instantly injected a touch of romance. His origins could not have been more ordinary; but with his love of fantasy he played up to the fairy tales and he embroidered richly on the legends which his appearance evoked. Towards the end of his life, however, he began to reveal the true facts of his origin to those who came to interview him, realizing that biographical details are an essential part of literary criticism, that they help to place an author in his times and to trace the influences brought to bear on his work and its development.

But it is impossible to draw a living picture of a man whom one has never met and the account of his life is here intended as a background to his writing which has not received sufficient serious attention from literary critics. James Stephens could start no school of writing. Both prose and poetry were the expression of his own individual personality and the literary theories he evolved were too general in character to cause any revolution. His critical sense was sound but his criticism was telling simply for the way in which it was written, and an analysis of much of his work shows that it contains just what another writer would not be bothered with—conversations between two children and a leprechaun, greetings and comments on normal everyday chores, or the thoughts of a weary donkey after the day's work. The worth of such writing lies in the personality of its creator and it could produce nothing but imitation. He stood alone, refreshing in the delight he took in every small event that came to his notice. Some of his work of course has dated, but the best has not, and it is the important bridge between the first Irish writers of the Celtic Twilight period and the new, more sophisticated writers.

The interest that this book has inspired has been most heartening and indeed it would have come to nothing had Stephens's friends and readers not so eagerly expressed a wish to see an account of his life in print and contributed what they knew with such determination. It is merely the opening volume in Stephens criticism, for many will come who will write with greater understanding than I; but I do think it important that an Irish person should offer an interpretation of his work, for while Stephens himself encouraged the leprechaun legend, it was the paradoxical quirk of a creative personality, and he regretted that so many of his readers regarded what he wrote as fantasy alone.

I cannot thank properly all those who have offered information for use in this work. In particular I should like to mention: H. Annett, Mrs. H. Archer, the late Dr. R. I. Best, Miss E. Bodkin, Mrs. T. Bodkin, John Brennan, Miss D. Casserley, Austin Clarke, Mrs. T. Collins, T. C. Collins, Pádraic Colum, Miss C. Cullen, Dr. C. P. Curran s.c., T. S. C. Dagg, Miss E. Duncan, Laurence Easterbrook, Mrs. M. Farrell, Seán Ford, Mrs. Andrew Ganly, Dr. Monk Gibbon, Lady Glenavy, Mrs. A. Gregory, the late Mrs. Arthur Griffith, Professor Denis Gwynn, Lady Hanson, T. R. Henn, Mrs. J. Hillyard, Miss Norah Hoult, Lady Huxley, Lady Iredell, John Irvine, Mrs. Sophie Jacobs, Miss Eleanor Knott, Seán MacBride, s.c., R. McCall, V. P. McDonagh, Dr. Thomas McGreevy, Sir Compton McKenzie, C. F. McLoughlin, the late Brinsley Macnamara, Mrs. E. McWhirter, the Meath Protestant School Fund, Mrs. T. G. Moorhead, Angus Morrison, Paul Scott Mowrer, Miss K. O'Hara, Colm O Lochlainn, Mrs. I. Peterkin, Miss Ruth Pitter, Reginald Pound, Miss Dilys Powell, W. J. Rafter, District Justice Kenneth Reddin, Cyrus F. Rice, Mrs. Lennox Robinson, P. Sayers, Dr. R. C. Simington, Mrs. Harley Lisle Sleith, Professor F. St. G. Sleith, Dr. Bethel Solomons, Mrs. S. Starkey, the late Mrs. Cynthia Stephens,

Preface

Colin Summerford, John M. Watkins, the late Professor H. O. White, Mrs. Iris Wise, Mrs. A. Wood. Many more have spontaneously co-operated, producing references and hunting out facts, but they have specially earned my gratitude for their encouragement and interest. I should like to thank Mr. Terence de Vere White for his kindness and patience in reading through a messy typescript when it was completed, my brother Fergus for practical assistance and continual encouragement and my sister for her insistence on the following up of new clues, for her enthusiasm and her help in typing out the manuscript. My thanks are also due to Mrs. Wise, to the Society of Authors and to Macmillan and Co., London, for permission to quote from Stephens's works and to reproduce his line-drawings.

Perhaps the most important fact that has come to light is how much James Stephens was esteemed and loved by all who knew him.

HILARY PYLE

PART ONE

Dublin — 1880 - 1925

The crooked paths go every way
    Upon the hill—they wind about
    Through the heather in and out
Of the quiet sunniness.
And there the goats, day after day,
    Stray in sunny quietness,
Cropping here and cropping there,
    As they pause and turn and pass,
Now a bit of heather spray,
    Now a mouthful of the grass.
                  The Goat Paths

I

Youth

The Dublin I was born to was poor and Protestant and athletic.
While very young I extended my range and entered a Dublin
that was poor and Catholic and Gaelic—a very wonderworld.
Then as a young writer I further extended to a Dublin that
was poor and artistic and political. Then I made a Dublin for
myself, my Dublin.

Memories of Dublin

TO be hailed as a fantasist and named the Leprechaun of
English Literature is surely not the ambition of one who wishes
to achieve eminence as a writer and yet in some curious
manner James Stephens seems to have welcomed the attitude
which shrouded his beginnings in myth. Indeed he deliberately
made a mystery of his birth and birthplace from the time that
he entered literary circles. He quoted a date for his birth only
when it acquired mystical significance through its coincidence
with that of James Joyce, and for most of his life he insisted that
a writer's life should be considered unimportant when approach-
ing his work. Before he died, however, he began to write his
autobiography and there is no reason to suppose that he would
not have completed it if he had lived longer. The fragment that
he published[1] gives no clue to the details of his origin. It is
pure story, related with enjoyment and interest in the story for
its own sake and not at all for its biographical import. Stephens's
style left no room for significant detail. From first to last he
upheld imagination, inspiration from a divine source, as the
basis of good writing.

Yet Gogarty and one or two others knew when Stephens was
born, and when we trace his beginnings it is evident that it was

[1] *Modern Irish Short Stories*. Selected with an introduction by Frank
O'Connor. (The World's Classics) 1957. By James Stephens: 'A Rhinoceros,
Some Ladies and a Horse.' 106–118.

3

purely on principle that Stephens made a mystery of his background, the principle that poetry and prose should be regarded with objectivity; he upheld this principle with great zest through a quirk of personality that revelled in a hint of drama. His childhood was unremarkable and the legends which later abounded were the result of the ability of the tiny man to spin an interesting tale from the most ordinary event and to draw a simple action with enthralling description. Where he inherited the gift we cannot say since public records have been started too recently for us to examine his ancestry.

His father, Francis Stephens, was a Dublin vanman, working as a messenger in Her Majesty's Stationery Office, who died of phthisis when his son was two years old. James Stephens remembered nothing of his father, and it was undoubtedly through ignorance with no intention to mislead that he referred to him as a bank clerk or a bank manager. His mother, Charlotte Stephens,[1] whose maiden name was Collins[1], may have shared her son's genius for storytelling. Stephens would have become sufficiently acquainted with her as an infant though she was probably inclined to neglect him. She was still Mrs. Charlotte Stephens in 1886, but Stephens has said more than once that she remarried and would have nothing more to do with him. This may not be strictly true, but she certainly appears to have been very uninterested in him. Then there was a brother, Francis, who was born in 1871,[2] and whom Stephens would have remembered if he had known him, but since he has never referred to a brother, and there is no record of his death as a boy one can only conjecture that he left home at an early age.

The Stephenses were married at Jervis Street Presbyterian Church on 27 January 1867, at which time Francis Stephens was an auctioneer's assistant. They lived in various houses in the

---

[1] Records of the Irish Department of Education, giving the date of Stephens's entry into the Meath School. The date of his birth has been traced from these records, where he is said to have been aged six in 1886. Charlotte Stephens's son, born in 1880, is described in the Dublin Register of Births as an 'unnamed male child'. This is the only Stephens born in the Dublin area in 1880, and no Stephens was born on 2 February 1882.

[2] His birth was registered by his mother on 9 November 1871. She gave his name as Francis, born on 9 August 1871, the son of Francis Stephens, 13 Grenville Street, and Charlotte Maria Stephens, formerly Collins; profession of father store keeper (?).

4

centre of Dublin. They were living in Grenville Street when Francis was born; at 5 Thomas Court, off the broad Thomas Street by St. Catherine's Church, when James was born on 9 February 1880 (he always claimed, nevertheless, to have been born on the same day as James Joyce, 2 February 1882); and they had moved to 5 Artigan's Dwellings, off Buckingham Street, when the elder Francis Stephens died on 6 May 1882. Here records cease for the moment, and imagination only can fill in the background of their life of poverty; the narrow streets of dilapidated Georgian houses with crowded slum dwellings, the crush and jostling in too little space, and up and down the narrow staircases during the day, ten or twelve, perhaps more, stretching to sleep in the shabby room at night.

James Stephens and his mother were living at 8 St. Joseph's Road, Prussia Street, between the Cattle Market and Grange Gorman Asylum, when he left her to go to school. He was six years of age, and had been committed to the Meath School for begging in the streets. He may not have been begging, but merely wandering alone, which at the time was regarded equally as an offence; but to families of the impoverished classes such a sentence was regarded as an achievement, for the Meath School gave a sound basic education and practical training as a clerk or craftsman. Many mothers sent their sons out to beg pennies from passersby so that they might qualify for entrance. After this Stephens may never have seen his mother again. He said that she abandoned him at the age of three; and it may be that he stayed with some other family and when going to school was registered in her name only because she was still living. Certainly he did not return to her when he was discharged from the Meath School.

The Meath Protestant Industrial School for Boys had been opened in May 1871. It owed its foundation to the Earl of Meath, who suggested at a meeting of the Board of the Heytesbury Female Protestant Industrial School that a school similar to the Heytesbury School[1] should be started for boys since there was no Protestant Industrial school for boys in the province of

---

[1] This must be the Industrial School for Protestant Females, 2 Heytesbury Street, Dublin, mentioned in Thom's Directory for 1870. The Meath Hospital extended from No. 1 to No. 9 Heytesbury Street so the Heytesbury School appears to have occupied part of the Meath Hospital building.

Leinster, or for that matter in Ulster or Connaught. He made the suggestion in January 1871, and five months later the first few inmates of the Meath School were installed in a house named Elmcliff in Blackrock, County Dublin. 'The object of these schools,' read the first report of the school committee, 'is to afford a refuge, and to give a Scriptural and industrial education to young children in cases where, either by the neglect or vice of their parents, they are driven on the streets to beg, or where they are left homeless and exposed not merely to misery and want but to every temptation to crime.'

The excellence of the school quickly established itself. The lease at Elmcliff expired in May 1876, and the following April the school moved to Carysfort Avenue, Blackrock, to a building capable of holding 100 boys. Soon the school was full and many applicants were being turned away each year. In addition to the normal curriculum of reading, writing and simple arithmetic there were excellent woodwork, shoemaking and tailoring classes, so that each boy would have a trade, and these were served by a visiting master tailor and master carpenter. A farm workman ran the farm with the aid of the boys and the school was virtually self-supporting. They had cows and livestock, and they owned a donkey and cart; and the top scholar, who held an enviable position, would bring the donkey and cart into Dublin from time to time to collect 'grains' from a brewery to feed the cattle.

The great grey building must have been imposing with the playing-fields spreading in front of it and a view of the Dublin Mountains to the west. Down a winding path, standing a little way away from it was the comfortable-looking hospital building with the Matron in charge. A Mr. Vanston was headmaster when Stephens was there, a man with a big black beard. He ran the school with rigid Victorian discipline, but old boys remembered the Meath School sufficiently favourably to visit it at intervals, and the pupils had a certain degree of freedom, being permitted to go out for short periods with responsible friends or relatives. Their uniform, of brown tweed, worn with a glengarry cap, was not too institutional.

Every boy in the school was known by a number. Stephens was No. 279. He was batman to an older boy, Harry Annett, No. 351, who came to the school a short time later. This was

6

fortunate for Stephens. Annett proved a great favourite with Mr. Vanston, who made him a monitor and made him largely responsible for the school library and school records. Annett's mother visited him and his brother regularly, bringing books for them to read, such as *The Three Musketeers, Coral Island,* and Rider Haggard's *She* and also G. A. Henty's adventure books, and Stephens developed the habit of reading early. He was already a notable character and generally liked; Mr. Johnston gave him the nickname of 'The Fiddler' for his play-acting, and immediately he was known by this name throughout the school.

Though Mr. Vanston was headmaster, and ran the school well, he was more interested in books than administration, and the school was largely under the influence of the military Mr. Johnston. Mr. Johnston organized a brass band, which became so highly regarded that it was soon in demand at all local functions. However, by Stephen's time the Board had decided that it must be reserved for gatherings which concerned the school alone.

Every Sunday morning the boys would form a crocodile and march down Carysfort Avenue, accompanied by the music of the band, on their way to church. The names of the boys who were pumping the organ may still be seen carved in the loft of Carysfort Church. Stephens later told a story of how he was brought to sing in the choir of a Protestant church as a boy. 'Looking down from the choir one day at the rows of men's heads and ladies' hats below him he was suddenly overcome with a sense of the ridiculous. He burst into such uncontrollable laughing that he was forcibly thrown out and never allowed to return.'[1] This story may be apocryphal, but it indicates how solid Victorian Protestantism affected him and inclined to poison his mind against the conventional. He also remarked on several occasions that he remembered Protestant hymns with distaste. Of course his Presbyterian background would have been responsible for this too.

James Stephens's closest friends at the Meath School were Tom Collins, who was about the same age as himself, and Tom's younger brother Dick. The Collins family lived at 8 Albert Road, Kingstown, and the father was stated to be in poor health, so in 1891 both sons were admitted to the Meath

[1] Denis Gwynn (*Cork Examiner*), 17 July 1959.

School. Gymnastics were an important item in the school curriculum and a fine training was provided. Their love of athletics formed a bond between somewhat diverse characters: Tom was tall, fair and active, his dark-haired brother was similarly built, and the small gnome-like Stephens, with his strong wiry arms, was a natural gymnast. The brothers were intelligent and fond of reading and they sympathized with Stephens's scribbling, and used to save the paper pokes off a 'hap'orth' of sweets for him to write his tales on.[1]

In general the boys stayed at the Meath School until they were sixteen when a great many went into the British Army, and others were apprenticed to various trades. Tom Collins left school in October 1895, and obtained employment with Mr. G. Armstrong, a house furnisher and plumber. Six months later, on 30 April 1896, James Stephens was discharged and sent to a post as junior clerk with Mr. Wallace, a solicitor, at 9 Eustace Street. Dick Collins left some time afterwards to go to a similar position. Stephens had become very friendly with the Collinses while at school and had been in the habit of accompanying them when they went home to stay with their mother, who had now moved in to Dublin, to York Street. He had been spending so much time there that Mrs. Collins, a woman of character who, even when over eighty, is said to have had coal-black hair, invited him to come and live with them when he left school. It was surely a moment of jest, but Stephens took the suggestion seriously; and he fitted into the Collins household well, being full of fun and of a happy disposition, and Mrs. Collins treated him as one of her own sons.

At the time that Stephens was living there most of York Street was in flats and it was extremely shabby. The Collinses occupied rooms at the better end of the street. The Knott family lived opposite. Mrs. Knott used to act as chaperone to young ladies who were coming out; and it was one of the delights of the Collins household to stand in the street at the beginning of each new season and watch the carriages moving off from her door on their way to parties at the Castle. Doctors and dentists and other professional men owned houses near by and John Butler Yeats had his studio there. No. 30 still had fine mahogany doors and a respectable appearance. It was a full house and a lively

[1] Mrs. Tom Collins.

one. In the front parlour on the second floor (the windows of which are reputed never to have been open) lived the Collinses and Stephens and Jim Foley, who worked in Eason's but later decided to emigrate to America. Jim Foley was very tall and charming. The incongruity in their heights was remarkable but he and James Stephens became great friends and went about together a great deal. To distinguish him from his friend Stephens was called 'Tim' or Tiny Tim.

Upstairs on the next floor lived the Whelans and the Sharkey family. Daisy Sharkey, the second eldest daughter, was an invalid and Jim Foley and 'Tim' used to come up and amuse her with their chatter and joking. She told them one day that the jollifications of the Collins family in the room below sounded like a wake. Next morning she was removed to hospital and she died of acute rheumatic fever on the following day. She was only twenty-one.

Stephens was friendly too with the Cullens, cousins of the Sharkeys, who were living next door, in No. 29. One of the Miss Cullens, who was about the same age as Stephens, accompanied him to a musical comedy at the Gaiety one night. He had only one penny and a half-crown with which to entertain the young lady. An orange woman was selling fruit outside the theatre and he bought an orange for them to suck. To his horror he discovered, when they reached their seats in the gods, that he had given the half-crown in payment for the orange. He dashed downstairs panic-stricken and was filled with joy when the kind-hearted woman gave the half-crown back to him.

All through his life Stephens approached children with sympathy and interest, and it was one of his pleasures to play with the younger Cullens, Sharkeys and Whelans. He used to perform acrobatics to amuse them and then when he wished to be alone set them running races, offering a prize of chocolate. He would give them any spare pennies he had to buy twists of sweets. The scraps of paper in which the sweets were purchased were in fact well used, and he would also beg white wrapping paper from the grocer's shop on which to write his first attempts at stories and poems; these were carefully stored in a tin box, but a member of the family mistook them for rubbish and burned them. Stephens sent one of his early stories to George

9

Bernard Shaw to ask for his opinion and received a disparaging reply on a postcard, which he treasured faithfully.

Neither Stephens nor his friends remained long in their first positions, but they moved from place to place and gradually became proficient in typewriting. Stephens also taught himself shorthand. Once he and Tom Collins applied for temporary posts as office boys in Harry Annett's office,[1] Maffett's, in South Frederick Street. Mr. Murphy, the book-keeper, was an entertaining old man who talked about the rebellion of 1867 a great deal; and in one anecdote he told them how the military cut the buttons off the rebels' trousers as they captured them so as to hinder their escape. Mr. Murphy wore a tall hat which took the fancy of the mischievous boys. One day for a joke they painted it inside with gum so that when he put it on it stuck to his head. Stephens held many similar positions in solicitors' offices before he settled down permanently. One firm, Finch and Clieff, he renamed 'Clinch and Thief'. He worked too for a Mr. Vanston, as far as is known no relative of the headmaster of the Meath School, whose wife was a sculptress and practised as a medium; and her conversation may have excited the youthful Stephens to dabble in esotericism.[2] Be that as it may, his varied experience and observation built up a store of impressions on which his imagination drew. He did not only depend on practical experience. He seized every book upon which he could lay his hands, and in the summer evenings was constantly to be seen seated in the back garden or legs stretched along the area wall, unconscious of the outer world as he read.

In their free time he and the other boys would often form cycling parties and go out to Bray or Kingstown and Stephens's buffoonery was frequently in evidence. He was also eager to inject an element of the ridiculous into gymnastic practice, which they kept up after leaving school. On winter evenings, James and Tom and Dick, with one of the Sharkeys, would go

[1] Mr. Annett.

[2] He also worked as a shorthand-typist at Richard Dickeson's, 18 Upper Exchange Street, but the date is unknown. Dickeson's were caterers to the army, and the manager was Mr. Doubleday, a big stout man. The head clerk was Mr. Jenkins, the cashier was Mr. Toogood, and the man in charge of the distribution of the mineral waters was Mr. Dover. James Stephens is said to have been quiet and reserved and he hardly ever opened his mouth. He wore a shabby dark-brown suit and a big collar to hide his goitre. He was a very efficient shorthand-typist. (W. J. Rafter).

down to the gymnasium in the Engineers' Hall in 8 Dawson Street. James was so agile that when the table was laid for a meal he would vault from one side to the other without grazing a vessel, merely placing his hands on the edge. He could also hold his leg upright, parallel to his body. His arms were long, though as an adult his full height never exceeded four foot ten inches, and a hope of improving his small stature and physical puniness encouraged the practice of gymnastic exercises. He said once that his first ambition had been to become an acrobat, light, swift and strong, 'like one of Dan Lowry's acrobats on the Olympia stage'.

In 1901 he joined the Y.M.C.A., rejoicing in the well-stocked library that availed itself,[1] and in the same year he and Tom were chosen as members of the Dawson Street Gymnastic Club team. The Dawson Street Gymnasium was well-fitted with a vaulting horse, parallel bars and climbing ropes, and the Club had a wide reputation, also enjoyed in free gymnastics. Their only rival in Ireland was the Sackville Gymnasium. The famous Christian family, or 'Christian Brothers', as they were known, and some of the other members often travelled to England and Scotland to competitions. The eldest of the four Christians was captain of the team that year.

Stephens and Collins must have attained a high standard of gymnastics, for their team was entered for the 'Irish Shield', presented by a Mr. J. C. Nutting, D.L., which was a valuable trophy, and carried with it medals for individual winners and runners-up. The draw for shields took place in January and the City of Dublin and Belfast teams were designated for the first round of 'The Irish Shield'. On 11 February Dawson Street Gymnasium competed against Inchicore. There were four stages, accompanied by music at the piano; bar-bells, which were arranged in squads; rings; jumping; and rope. The final took place between Dawson Street and the Dublin Gymnasium Club, at the Earlsfort Terrace Rink on 21 March. Here the

[1] In the Library Loan Book, P. Stephens of 30 York Street was a frequent borrower of novels and other books. Later, in 1901, his address is given as 14 Portobello Road, which may have been when he left the Collinses. In one case the 'P' is overwritten so as to appear as 'J'. Since the P is written in a curly script, might it be in fact 'S'? During his periods of enthusiasm for the Irish language Stephens preferred to be known by the Irish version of the name James, Seumas.

exercises employed rings, the horizontal bar and an arrangement for Indian clubs in a squad formation. 'The competition was somewhat close', the *Irish Times* reported, 'but the Dawson Street team was certainly superior.' Tom Collins and Stephens displayed the photograph of the winning team proudly on their mantlepieces for the rest of their lives, Tom appearing as a Hercules, knit with muscle, and Stephens posed in a romantic reclining attitude, without the slightest suggestion of a twinkle in his eye.

Stephens's life was passed in the manner conventional for those of his class in the Dublin of that day. They lived from hand to mouth in bare unfurnished lodgings, pinching and scraping, with occasional spells of luck. They eked fun out of any situation that occurred, and relied to a great extent on the goodwill of friends, who also appreciated a helping hand from time to time. The Collinses had a deep affection for the young boy and loved him in excited or in clowning mood. He was a delightful companion, peaceful, loquacious or singing. They were intrigued by his active pen.

But about that time Stephens realized that further experience was necessary for him and that his horizon should be extended in order to give him subject matter and a chance to develop an individual style of writing. His feeling that a writer's life bore no relation to his work promoted ideas of self-sacrifice and of dedication to his craft; and the decision in 1901 to leave his friends, for ever, was born of a wish to become great in the literary field. It may not have been his first separation from them, for in between jobs he may have ventured farther afield, perhaps accompanied by one of the other boys. Whether it was before 1901 or not is difficult to tell, as at an early stage he walked from Dublin to Belfast looking for a job, and according to George Moore, he would have perished in Belfast had it not been for a charitable apple-woman. He worked there as a bread-server, delivering bread to people's houses. Another source reports that he travelled about the countryside on the back of a cart, selling turf, and the form of *The Demi-Gods* tends to verify this story. There is doubt as to whether the games listed by the Leprechaun in *The Crock of Gold* are Dublin games,[1] which are all that Stephens would have known at first hand,

[1] Mrs. Dillon thinks they belong to some area north of Dublin.

unless he had travelled. On the other hand he may have associated at school with a boy from the provinces before attaching himself to Tom and Dick Collins. The rumour about Belfast, however, is sufficiently widespread to be credited with truth and only the date is elusive. Another story, which may be believed, belongs to the period after he left the Collinses—his own tale of how, with tramps and other vagrants, he used to conceal himself within the gates of St. Stephen's Green after dark and attempt to catch the ducks, without success; though this may have been a single occasion, enhanced through pretence of frequency. He was quick, too, to introduce a touch of humour into any reminiscences. He told one friend that as a boy he bought a pair of bicycle clips so that it might be supposed that he owned a bicycle.

Glimpses of the poet's background may be seen and greatly assist in a study of his work, which might otherwise merely scratch the surface. In the early years of the century he found a post in a solicitor's office, Reddington and Sainsbury, in Upper O'Connell Street. R. C. Simington,[1] who was also working there, found the new clerk entertaining and a fine conversationalist. Both were writing secretly, unknown to the other,[2] but they had many literary conversations and lent each other their books. The first that Stephens recommended to his colleague was Plato's *Republic*. They often discussed religion, and Stephens insisted that religions would not exist were it not for death, for he was going through a period of disillusionment after the rigidity of his Protestant upbringing. He still exercised regularly, with vain hope, and he taught his fellow employee some exercises for good health which he had found in a book. During their acquaintanceship he often referred to the poverty of his childhood, a condition with which the other young man was familiar and could sympathize. He had once to fight with a dog for a loaf of bread when desperate for a mouthful of food, he said. When he was destitute he was taken in by a prostitute without knowing about her profession, and she looked after him with great compassion. According to another version of the story, he threw himself into the Liffey one night full of despair

[1] Now Dr. R. C. Simington.
[2] They both published in *Sinn Féin*, Dr. Simington under the pseudonym Robert Barry', Stephens under his own name.

that the first of his books had not been accepted by any publisher, but on reaching the water he had second thoughts and struck out for the bank. A prostitute who was passing took him home and gave him a bed and food until he recovered.

The stories that Stephens told to his friends were related for their entertainment value and with no thought at the time that his biography would one day be of interest; and dealt with in this manner they find no place in a chronology. One can theorize, as his friends did, and attempt to pin down the events of his youth *ad infinitum,* but it is clear at least that his early life was more conventional than he led people to believe and unmarked by notable incident. Perhaps enough is known of the atmosphere of his background to illuminate his character and work. In 1901, anyway, he altered his address, as we see from the Library Loan Book of the Y.M.C.A. in Dawson Street, and went to live in lodgings in Portobello Road. Later still he lived near Essex Street. The Collinses never heard from him again, or had any news from him other than a copy of *The Crock of Gold* which arrived eleven years after he left them. They thought that he had emigrated to America, but oddly enough they sensed no ingratitude. For an emotional man of fine perceptions, such as Stephens, a period of detachment and independence was essential and when he had benefited from its effect he entered the Dublin literary world in his own right.

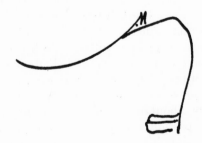

II

Early Writings

His own story was that he became a writer due to his stature. His first job was driving a horse and cart around Dublin, but he could not stand the contempt of the horses for one who had to stand on a box to harness them. He discovered that the only thing he could do without being at a disadvantage was to write.
Gerard Fay: *Irish Times*, 18 January 1961

MYSTERY shrouds the next few years, and that is how Stephens would have it. He is next heard of in a permanent post which provided sustenance until he was able to support himself with his own writing. In 1906 he started work as a clerk-typist in Messrs. Mecredy, 91 Merrion Square, at a salary of 20*s*. a week. He quickly made his mark on the staff of the office, for his gentle and curious individuality was already asserting itself. All about his desk on the wallpaper were tiny drawings of animals, 'never imagined on land or sea',[1] which he executed during his hours of work, and this habit of doodling remained with him all through his life. His appearance too was distinctive. He had never grown. His diminutive stature was dominated by a large impressive head with receding forehead and a shock of black hair like a golliwog. A shabby dark-brown suit served for all purposes, topped by a tall collar to hide his goitre. He smoked a large briar pipe with a bent shank. The bowl of the pipe was worn away with constant knocking out of the dottle, and it was a cause of general amazement that it held tobacco at all.

He had long left the Dawson Street Gymnasium, but he still practised athletic exercises with fervour, and was exceedingly active. Each evening, he would bounce down the stairs from his top-floor office, six at a time, like a rubber ball, and do a little step-dance at the end of each flight. He was competent at

[1] Val McDonagh, who was employed in the same office.

15

his work and had a photographic memory, according to a contemporary, so that his transcription of letters was accurate; but he had no interest in the law, and in other respects he was not an efficient clerk.

It is not surprising that Stephens was not wholly given to his work, for he was determined that he would be a writer. The year before, in 1905, he had appeared for the first time in print in the pages of *The United Irishman*.[1] On his own evidence he was caught up in the movement of the Irish Revival, excited by thoughts of national independence and indignant over the neglect of the mother tongue. But he was very much on the fringe and his friends, who were equally moved, belonged to the interested mass who as yet contributed nothing.

'The Greatest Miracle' is an essay in short-story writing, untouched by political intent. The scene is laid in a crowded thoroughfare; the time, evening. Clerks and businessmen return home wearily and unnoticed, as every day. Everything is in order; and the big policeman watches complacently. All that concerns him is that the Law reigns, and he basks in the reflection that he is responsible. Suddenly the atmosphere changes. The policeman is uncomfortably disturbed. He sees a tramp, misshapen, ragged, bowed, limp into view. Immediately his world is shaken and he sees that there may be aspects of life outside that which he had hitherto accepted.

The prose style throughout the story is derivative and lacking in personality, and it bears no resemblance to the mature Stephens. But in the final passages the idealistic description of the worn-out man could belong to no one else:

He moved his feet with evident pain, as if he did a momentary duty for Atlas, and lifted the world at every step.

But above the wretched footsteps, shoulders, and the hopeless fluttering rags, about the half-opened mouth glowed and flickered a smile which shone with such a glorious radiance that the short red hair was transformed into the shining aura of some immortal being, and his eyes shone like stars.

The whole man, with all his wretchedness, was but a background for the radiant joy of that face.

Almost it seemed that the very misery of his apparel was but

---

[1] 'The Greatest Miracle' (*United Irishman*), 16 September 1905.

a symbol of the thinness of that veil which divided the world wherein he *existed* from the world in which he *lived.*

As if he were even now upon the shining borderland of 'that country which he had always longed to see'.

'Joy', to which the tramp had attained, was Imagination in action, a conception which was to form the basis of Stephens's philosophy for life and work, though its ecstasy was toned down in later years to a vibrant peace. Here, the effect the tramp's radiance produced was added with glee, for Stephens deplored policemen: 'In the mind of the policeman that "greatest of miracles" had happened, a thought had come to birth.'

Stephens was writing on every conceivable subject to give himself practice, and it is a pity that more of these early pieces were not published and have not survived in any form; at this time and in the Sinn Féin period fluency was unabated and his faculty of self-criticism did not so predominate that it sapped the sources of his creative imagination. He benefited much from listening to the intellectual conversation of the Sleith family of Palmerston Park, and he was encouraged in particular by Mrs. Sleith. Perhaps he met her first through his employer, Mr. Mecredy. Mrs. Sleith had a musical evening every Sunday, and here was the opportunity for meeting many interesting people. The 'Brilliant Poem Polished by hand and Jas Stephens' may have arisen out of some fun at their house one night, when a legend was spun about 'Stout Friar Wright's' ill-luck:

> Stout Friar Wright in a doleful plight
> By the shell starr'd shore he tramped
> For his cossack & gown some villainous clown
> Had stolen from him & decamped.

This 'spasm done in twitches' as Stephens described it continues for some twenty good-humoured verses, spelt none too well, and they must have been the cause of great hilarity when recited for the first time. More important is the only surviving letter of this period, written to Mrs. Sleith when she was on holiday. Stephens had discovered a book on music in his lodgings and, fired by the performances he heard every Sunday evening, set out to teach himself how to play the piano. The results of his attempt at self-tutoring were described in faithful, rueful detail to his friend:

25 July 1906

Dear Mrs. Sleith,

Thanks for your postcard. It is a very pretty one. I am sorry that it should be so wet during your vacation. King Edward may be the monarch of this country but he cannot rain over it like King Cloud, and my very heart bled when I heard of the Boss having a puncture. I've been there so often myself that I am sorry for the Man who is not blasphemous by nature and is also handicapped by having his daughter with him.

But I also am in desperate straits. Know that a day or so back I discovered in the sequestration of the back parlour of the house which I infest, a piano, and subsequently a piano tutor written by a wandering Jew by the name of Hemy—This Hemy knows nothing about music—I'm sure he wears his hair short. First, do you see, he lured me gently into learning treble notes, all of which stood with their heads up—Then he hoisted another set of treble notes on me, with their heads down—That was pure cussedness on his part I'm certain, and then the ruffian insisted that I should play the notes that stood on their heads with my left hand, a thing that my left hand disdained to do—and that my right hand should meander royally over the notes that held their heads up like soldiers & men in the meantime, and then this Hemy flabbergasted me with an infernal assortment of what he called 'Leger' notes that were ringstraked speckled & spotted like Joseph's coat—The perverted ingenuity of this man is marvellous—I'm just certain that he knows more about hods than pianos. Imagine, Mrs. Sleith, when the third finger of my right hand was flattening out 'F' this man expected the first finger of my *left* hand to perform 'F' at the other end of the room—He may know something about music, but he certainly knows nothing about my left hand—My hands are a scriptural sort of hands, the right hand never knows what the left hand is doing—and then the note 'C'. Hit it says Hemy with the thumb of your right hand and the little finger of your left—Hit it with my hat and my socks, I assure I could'nt hit it with anything—Do you see, in order to hit it with my right thumb I've got to gently but firmly coerce my right thumb on to that note, first finding out where the misfortunate note is, and Hemy thinks that while I'm battling with my right thumb my left little finger is going to play on 'C'. My left little finger

has too much pride to do anything of the kind, it's engaged punching a black note somewhere on the horizen—Hit em both at the same time, says Hemy, but when my right thumb has discovered 'C' I've got to count back from it till I find 'C' for my little finger, and besides, when I do hit with my left hand I hit four notes all at once or maybe kill an octave—it's a terrible ambitious hand that—and then, when I have found the left hand 'C' and am holding my little finger down with my foot I become painfully aware that my right thumb has got on to 'F' and the problem of how to get it back and still hold my left little finger where it should be is a very distressing thing. When I am nonplussed I want to scratch my head, and I always scratch my head with my left hand and if I scratch my head with my left hand I lose my 'C' and if I dont I lose my wits and meantime my thumb is prodding foolishly at 'G' and if I'd get a grip on Hemy I'd get in the left hand as well. The villian has just turned bass notes on to me, altogether different from the ones I learned with the sweat of my brow and some of these have their heads up and some of them have their heads down and then there are more ringstraked Leger notes, and what my left hand little finger is going to do about it is beyond either me or Hemy. I feel as if my hands were ten times as big as the piano, the notes look like miscroscopic foolishness, my head seems filled with putty and my heart with hatred and despair, hatred of Hemy—the infamous Hemy—and despair of ever meeting him in the flesh and playing a rollentando on his 'C' (eyes)— Pray for me Mrs. Sleith for I sorely need the intervention of Providence to prevent myself going mad, thinking I am a note and trying to hand myself up on a butchers scales. I am sending some books on to the Boss later on. Love to yourself and the youngsters. If there is any bad spelling in this letter put it down to love—Of course, I'm wildly, madly in love with you and I never could be in love and spell right at the same time.
Yours with rolling eyes and detestation of Hemy

James Stephens

P.S. I have not yet discovered the No. of the house where I am stopping.
P.P.S. I died last night longing for roast pork. I intend to die twice on Sunday night of the same complaint.
P.P.P.S. A jewsharp is my mark. P.P.P.S. SS—x—

Stephens is at his best as he is here, caught unawares, and one can imagine him rolling the words off his lips with enjoyment, scarcely giving his pen time to transmit them to paper.

In 1906 or 1907 Stephens met Arthur Griffith, an event which marked the beginning of his career as an Irish writer. Perhaps his article in the *United Irishman*, 'The Greatest Miracle', had brought him to the notice of the great patriot and started their life-long friendship, though if it did attract Griffith's attention it is curious that he did not accept anything more from Stephens for the *United Irishman* or for *Sinn Féin* when it first started. Stephens's articles on nationalism appear so regularly in *Sinn Féin* from 1907 on that they were probably a series by special arrangement. The two men may have been introduced at a Gaelic League meeting and launched into a discussion on Irish politics, or Stephens may have offered his first article to Griffith in April 1907 and discovered that it was exactly what Griffith wanted. However they met, it was from Griffith that Stephens adopted his pacifist views on nationalism, and his devotion to the Irish language as Ireland's only method of gaining her freedom was stimulated by Griffith as well. Griffith's encouragement and regular publishing of his articles brought him to the notice of the foremost writers in Dublin and within a few years he had achieved international recognition.

Arthur Griffith had trained as a compositor and then spent some years in Africa before returning to Ireland, determined to use every weapon in his power to free his country from English domination. In appearance he was short and square-cut. His achievement was to be revolutionary, yet he was conservative in character, quiet and retiring and uninterested in social events, and it would have been difficult to believe that he was to be the first President of the Irish Free State. This was a man who was admirably suited to act as personal secretary to a leader but who had neither ambition, stamina, nor the distinction of personality to fill a position of eminence himself. Yet Griffith's dogged determination put the movement for political freedom on a firm footing and his clear-headed approach might have fulfilled the wish of so many without bloodshed, and the resulting bad feeling, had it not been for the panic at the time of the Great War.

Griffith's satirical pen was powerful, and the indomitable obstinacy with which he refused to be silenced was invaluable to Irish nationalism. Politics and letters were inextricably linked in the Ireland of his day. Though he had no literary pretensions himself, he was Secretary to the Celtic Literary Society for a time and he was eager to encourage young Irish writers.

The Abbey Theatre was not the sole instrument for promoting Irish writing, as distinct from the offshoot of English literature exemplified in rather sentimental nineteenth-century ballads. The Gaelic League, founded in 1893, had interested Edward Martyn in Irish as a medium for the stage, and when Yeats and Lady Gregory wished to counteract Ibsen's realism and went to native Irish folklore and epic for their symbolism, they readily called on Douglas Hyde to contribute short plays in the Irish tongue for performance in the Abbey, Hyde, who composed lyric poetry, in some cases providing the language (Irish literally translated into English) in the plays and Lady Gregory the dramatic construction. George Russell, better known by his pen-name, A.E., was not a dramatist either, but he was drawn for a time into the Irish National Theatre Society, and became one of the Vice-Presidents. The clash inevitable among creative personalities led to his withdrawal; and conscience over public matters interested him in the organization of co-operative banks, and co-operative schemes for Irish farmers, while he indulged his private bent publishing *The Irish Homestead*.

Griffith did not merely see this new literary movement as a means to political ends and in his weekly publication *The United Irishman*, started in 1899, writers, as well as future politicians, made their début, Seumas O'Sullivan, Alice Milligan and John Eglinton among others. *The United Irishman* was suppressed in 1906 for its revolutionary tendencies and it sprang up again instantly as *Sinn Féin*; and when censors attacked the latter he produced *Scissors and Paste*, a compilation of accidentally relevant quotations from extraneous sources, which brought home the poignancy of the Irish question.[1]

Stephens published regularly in Griffith's paper, writing idealistic verses, essays on poetry and ethics, and propaganda

[1] *United Irishman* ran from 4 March 1899 to 14 April 1906; *Sinn Féin* from 5 May 1906 to 28 November 1914; *Scissors and Paste* from 12 December 1914 to 27 February 1915. *Sinn Féin* also ran as a daily newspaper from 24 August 1909 to 21 January 1910.

for the Sinn Féin party. His prose articles showed the greatest promise in style and content. He felt that freedom for Ireland was the very natural desire of her countrymen and that it was not ungrateful to reject England. English laws are suited to England and work admirably there, having been nurtured on English soil, and by the English race, but they are totally unsuited to Ireland's needs. In 'The Seoinin', the first of his articles,[1] the contempt of the average Irishman for Irish goods and traditions was detestable to him;

> Good clothes for him generally argues a good accent, and any grocer's curate from Manchester who visits this country for a week's vacation in order to study the habits of the wild Irishry in their native bogs is generally accepted by the Seoinin as a shining intellectual star and a model of gentlemanly deportment. Our distinguished visitor dilates on the magnificence of England, the 'w'ite walls h'of of h'old h'England', and remarks, as the result of his first evening's dissipation, that 'you h'Irish h'if you were not', or perhaps, was not—'so drunken in yr 'abits and so dispritely iggerent in your 'eads, wouldn't be 'aff a bad sawt', and the Seoinin smiles approval, not understanding that the man has just insulted him and everything that is his.

He blamed the 'suicidal system' of education for this sense of inferiority. English songs, history, literature and language were being taught in schools, and the Irish way of life based on a diluted and inferior form of English life. Worst of all, he lamented, in his next article, 'Builders', on 11 May 1907, Ireland accepted the false way in which England represented her to the European countries as backward and filled with a race of malformed savages. Stephen's fierceness in this last point echoed Swift's 'Yahoo' satire. He advocated a less passive attitude to nationalism and in this, and in a later article, 'Irish Englishmen', he called for greater co-operation between North and South in the fight for independence. He urged the Northern Irish to forget religious differences in the past and to work for a future unity. Prejudices must be buried. His articles after these are in the same vein and they are very powerful and characteristic of his own directness as well as being full of his natural humour and understanding of human attitudes. In all of them he wished for less political cant and more sympathy and under-

[1] 20 April 1907.

22

standing between opposite parties. Hard work is the important thing, he said; too much time has been wasted in fruitless talk when a sounder national economy might have achieved. In 'To Mr. George Birmingham's "Asses"—an Epistle' there is something of the rhythm of Kipling in his energetic outburst:

> Get up an' scratch the country with a plough, or fist a hod,
> Work while y'iv got y'er arms an' lave the issue to your God;
> And don't sit round an' blather while yer counthry's on the
> shelf;
> I've heard it said 'God helps the lad that up's and helps
> hisself'.[1]

On 22 June, 1907, Stephens published an important article on poetry. His mode of expression was wholly individual and quite unlike usual methods of criticism; and, again, it altered little during his life. His practice was to dart around the subject pouring all the strength of emotion into it of which he was capable. In 'Poetry' he stated the belief which he upheld to the end of his life, that inspiration is the source of poetry. Poetry is not a contrived art initially, though it must be worked thoroughly. Imagination is at the root of great art and poetry is the greatest of the arts. He then enumerated further doctrines. The poet must devote himself to the realities of life, which have their foundations in simplicity:

> The joys and sorrows of man, the wondrous love of woman, the delight of victory, the bitterness of defeat, The brave Songs of the Sunlight, the sadly, sweet Verse of the Twilight, the dark, cold quietness of the Night Time, when the terrible bats go hunting, and the wonder of the big, dead Moon.

These emotions and experiences are basic to man. Wisdom, that is, understanding and sympathy, is the faculty with which the poet will approach them; and while any writer with enough intelligence is capable of mastering technique and practising observation, wisdom, without which these are of no avail, comes as a gift from God alone. Hard work is essential but above everything the poet must give all of himself. Stephens poured forth a panegyric of instruction, intense with the importance of his message:

[1] 4 January 1908.

He must not sing at the touching of a button, but with pain and the sweat of his brow, the way all good work is done. The Muse must be wooed with the passion of a lover. A cold heart never made a poem, nor a hot head either. Let our poet sing loudly. An eagle doesn't warble like a dickey bird. If you are a citizen of the Sun, don't look as if you lived in Tallow Candle Land. When you sing a love song, let the girl hear you. Sing of God and sing greatly. The World, the Flesh and the Devil are to your hands, and the Lust of the Flesh, the Delight of the Eye, and the Pride of Life are part of your human nature, clamant for expression—Sing the woe of the hunted rabbit when his legs begin to fail, and he hears the toothed devil close behind; and sing too, the joy of the dog when he leaps and feels the red, warm tide flush his throat. Battle, murder, and sudden death. Hope, effort, and escape. See it and understand it, and tell us of it. We will listen like little children to you if you are big enough to be listened to!

Stephens published poetry regularly in *Sinn Féin*. The idiom was traditional or colloquial. He had a fondness for Irish themes and the occasional word in Irish, for he was studying Father O'Growney's Irish grammar. He was also becoming interested in Irish legend. But these verses are slight and no more than exercises. Stephens knew this and did not republish them as he did his prose.

He loved Arthur Griffith and counted him as one of his few real friends. In his appreciation, written in 1922, he gave full due to Hyde's early efforts in arousing nationalist feeling, but Griffith, he felt, had been responsible for the practical achievement. Hyde had prepared the way for Griffith by upholding the Gaelic ideal. He had provided the ideal motive. Griffith had supplied 'the driving intelligence', and he had achieved more than political advance. 'Mr. Griffith's political campaign,' Stephens wrote, 'was certainly the most important cultural process that Ireland has undergone in recent times.' When his literary contributors failed him, he would produce articles on every topic and in any style. He was a shy, courageous, sensitive and generous man with a warm sense of humour. 'He is that most unusual of creatures,' Stephens wrote, 'a proud man with no vanity.'

Meeting 'Cynthia' contributed to the stable background necessary for his work, and certainly she was a source of inspiration to the writer. The story goes that Stephens took lodgings in the house of a couple named Kavanagh. This was probably in 17 Great Brunswick Street, from which place he addresses the poems written in 1908. Cynthia's husband, Mr. Kavanagh, has been described by different people as a shop-keeper, a sceneshifter and the doorkeeper of the Tivoli Theatre, a Dublin music-hall. He and Mrs. Kavanagh decided to part and he went off leaving his wife expecting a baby.[1] Stephens feared that he would compromise Mrs. Kavanagh if he remained in the house and he made arrangements to depart; but Mrs. Kavanagh insisted that she was without means and that she would prefer him to stay so that she would at least have his rent. James stayed and met all the expenses and gradually he made it known to his friends that he had a wife and family.

Millicent Josephine, to give Mrs. Kavanagh her real name, was a charming little person with red-gold hair, hazel eyes and a pink and white complexion. James renamed her after the moon, to him a symbol of religious significance, and she later adopted the name as her own. She had a strong personality. She could be overpowering. But Stephens was largely dependent upon her: she was infinitely kind and loyal and in his days of penury and ill-health she was a tower of strength. Stephens's deep affection for her is clear in the delightful portrait of Mary Makebelieve in *The Charwoman's Daughter*, where all the delightful traits are transcended and all the irritating characteristics are swept aside. For years they lived in a single room, with the children concealed behind a screen in the evening when people called, and here Cynthia made a comfortable home for James, arranging their few possessions tastefully. When they were most poor she made clothes for both of them with remarkable success.

Then in 1908 fame burst upon James Stephens and he realized that his contribution was recognized by those who had launched the literary movement. In *Hail and Farewell* Moore related how George Russell, A.E., looked for a rival to Yeats's discovery, Synge, and swore that he would find him in Arthur Griffith's paper; and there follows the description of A.E.'s

[1] Iris, now Mrs. Norman Wise, born *c.* 1908.

journey to Mecredy's office, when he had found his poet, his request to be introduced to Mr. Stephens, and the surprise when two big brown eyes looked up from the typewriter and the clerk answered, 'I am he.'

Stephens was not accepted by other writers immediately, however. He wrote of the occasion on which he justified the loyalty of those who espoused him, in his appreciation of Arthur Griffith in the *Review of Reviews*:

> When at one of our meetings that most learned of men, O'Connolly, once denied me any literary ability or common culture, and challenged me to recite even the four parts of speech correctly, I did so, itemizing them triumphantly as orthography, etymology, syntax and O'Connolly, and Griffith's joy was worth the tragic jest.

Gradually all barriers were removed and Stephens was expected to be in regular attendance at the Dublin literary evenings. He had met other contributors to Arthur Griffith's paper and the occasional interested person here and there; but he had only met intellectuals at Mrs. Sleith's house, and on a different footing. He had even been friendly outside the office with Mr. Mecredy's daughter who went to the Art School. Hilary Mecredy would drop in to the office occasionally to chat with him and he would offer his poems to her for criticism. But when he and his wife visited her family at 'Monte Vista', in Dalkey, he was shy of his employer, and the great gap between his employer's friends and himself that their social status occasioned made him diffident; Mecredy thoroughly disapproved of his writing and so his chief enjoyment on these visits had been to talk about poetry to young Miss Mecredy. Now a new world opened to him, 'a very wonderworld':

> Upon an evening I found myself sitting in the Bailey in front of a drink—I who had never yet drunk one. With me were Arthur Griffith, Tom Kettle, Oliver Gogarty, Seumas O'Sullivan, Seumas O'Connolly . . . I had my first adventure in that air, oxygen and gin, which we call wit, and which I watched, as a cat watches a mouse, meaning to catch it. And, for the first time, I heard poetry spoken of with the assured carelessness with which a carpenter talks of his planks and of the chairs and tables and oddments he will make of them.

It is hard for us to realize now the excitement of that time and the eagerness with which new talent was hailed. Desire for freedom was not new in Ireland. Men had died for their land before the English were firmly established and had been sacrificing themselves ever since; but now a fresh objective presented itself and ideas were powerful and growing. The Irish were to create a new Ireland which would sweep the foreigner out of their path, and back whence he came. The promotors of Young Ireland, the Nation, as distinct from the Sean Bhean Bhocht, or Poor Old Woman, who had existed in her wrongs and in the sufferings of her people, saw that the answer lay in 'Our Selves'. Heroes might at last attain their goal and eject the Sassenach instantly, but when they turned back in rejoicing might find but an empty shell and wonder what they had risked their lives for. So Hyde started the Gaelic League to revive and sustain the Irish language. Those who knew it could enjoy the company of other native speakers and the ignorant could listen to them; he recorded songs and poems that would otherwise have been lost. Yeats and Lady Gregory joined forces with the brothers Fay to found the national theatre where Irish and English might meet. Farmers were stimulated to co-operate with each other by A.E.'s and Plunkett's Agricultral Organization Society. On the literary side, daily, weekly, monthly and quarterly publications sprang up and when they disappeared there were others to replace them. The *New Ireland Review* was of a serious turn. Here Hyde first published his *Religious Songs of Connacht*, and other scholarly contributions and discoveries were printed, such as 'The True History of the Phoenix Park Murders'. Yeats wrote for *The Shanachie*, which included Eglinton's and Dunsany's work, Indian stories, poetry and articles on mysticism by James Cousins, poems by O'Sullivan, Susan Mitchell and Colum, translations of Turgenev and de Maupassant, and illustrations by Jack B. Yeats and his father. All this was the achievement of enthusiasts who were employed by day as accountants, clerks, electricians, lawyers and newspapermen, but were united in their single-hearted longing to free the true spirit of Ireland and give it all that they possessed. Finally Griffith bound literature and language with politics in his successive journals and in the live movement, Sinn Féin, whose branches spread all over the city. In the Sinn

Féin club rooms each week, there was a strong attendance whether for a political rally or a social evening with jigs, reels, set-dancing or recitation.

At the book carts in Aston Lane, on any Saturday morning, Griffith, H. E. Kenny (Sean Gall), Padraic Colum, O'Leary, Curtis and Seumas O'Connolly might be found, searching for material to feed their hungry minds and stimulate embryo ideas to growth. Discussion was rampant, and everyone was poised eagerly to hear anything new that had been written. Oliver Gogarty used to meet Stephens after work in the evenings and Stephens would recite some of the lyrics on which he had 'been sitting all day long in the office, keeping them warm like a hen on a nest of eggs'.

He too was caught up in the eagerness to create a new Ireland, and with his wife, or 'squaw' as he affectionately called her, went to the Gaelic League Irish classes and to ceilidhes, and he was a regular attendant at Sinn Féin meetings.

Concourse with other Dublin writers helped him to a degree of sophistication in his work which it had lacked hitherto. He would visit Seumas O'Sullivan with other young nationalists and writers, on Sunday mornings. Maud Gonne was At Home on Monday night; Colum had his house open on Tuesday evenings; Curran, and sometimes Stephens himself on Wednesday evenings; Sarah Purser had a stately afternoon soirée which was by invitation only, and it is unlikely that Stephens was ever there; on Saturday evenings Stephen MacKenna, later one of Stephens's closest friends, entertained; and on a Sunday evening A.E. held open house at his home in Rathgar Avenue. A.E. has often been described, sitting in the centre of a circle of admiring neophytes at his Hermetic Society, dressed in an open-necked shirt with his hairy chest showing. His evenings were conducted with as much ceremony. A.E. would come down and welcome each visitor personally and bring them up to the sitting-room. There would be a few Americans every time, for Russell's evenings were famous in Dublin. After tea and buns, at about ten o'clock, Mrs. Russell would say—'Your remark, George, today about the Ulster Question . . .' and for the rest of the evening there would be a monologue from A.E.

Seán O'Casey and Lennox Robinson have commented unkindly on the atmosphere, but O'Casey approved of

Stephens's allegiance to his friend on the occasions when Russell was in danger of looking ridiculous. Stephens was not daunted by A.E.'s pomposity. One evening, to A.E.'s astonishment, he asked the assembled company what had happened in 'Mutt and Jeff' that day. In the stunned silence he embarked on a nonsensical commentary of how this was modern American art in its early stages. A.E. was appalled and said that all such trash should be boiled in oil. A few weeks later, however, Stephens met him walking up Grafton Street bearing under his arm a bundle of papers containing back numbers of 'Mutt and Jeff', which he had had sent after him for his perusal to Donegal. Stephens and Russell also enjoyed detective stories and thrillers together, beginning their studies with M. P. Shiel. They amassed shelves full of them and exchanged them from time to time, delighting in the florid terms and incredibility.

It was not long before A.E. appeared in *Sinn Féin* under the title of the Old Philosopher. One of Stephens's favourite sayings was that a man never made more than six intimate friends during his lifetime. A.E. and Griffith were his first two intimate friends, yet he did not hesitate to make a gently humorous study of the former's pontification in his articles. The Old Philosopher discoursed on Washing, on Politeness, on Smoking, on Eating, and on Going to Bed, on Policemen, on Education and on a host of other subjects, on which A.E. must have lectured each Sunday evening, though here reinforced by Stephens's sympathetic imagination. The expression and wit are typically Stephens's, he made the subjects as much his as A.E.'s; and it is interesting to see that he did not merely record what he had noticed from watching, 'as a cat watches a mouse', but he moulded the material to his own purpose, achieving a finer result. He had already attempted character studies of 'Mrs. Maurice M'Quillan,' 'Old Mrs. Hannigan' and other people surely of his acquaintance, which were reprinted in *Here Are Ladies*, but these lacked the brilliance of the Old Philosopher's Discourses, from whence the Philosopher in *The Crock of Gold* was to originate. They appeared about twice a month from January 1909 onwards; some were reprinted in *Sinn Féin* and in *Here Are Ladies* and some in *The Crock of Gold*.

Stephens did not confine his free time to writing but joined the Theatre of Ireland Group. His miniature physique precluded type casting but characteristically he enjoyed this since it gave more scope to his gift of mimicry and for play-acting. In April 1909 he was cast as the hard-hearted chairman of a board of guardians in Seumas O'Kelly's play *The Schuler's Child*. Countess Marckiewicz and Máire Walker, or Máire Nic Shiubhlaigh as she preferred to be called, took part also. Stephens was taking the child away from the Schuler, Máire Walker, to place him in a home, and Máire had to throw herself at his knees to plead for mercy; but when she saw his face, made up as Mick McQuaid, the workhouse master of a current newspaper serial, she could not refrain from bursting into a peal of laughter. Her shoulders were shaking so much that the curtain had to be dropped. The play was a great success. Two years later, on 17 November 1911, his only play *The Marriage of Julia Elizabeth* (based on a short story) was performed by the Theatre of Ireland Group in Hardwicke Street. It was no more than a short story converted into a play, for Stephens was a story-teller, not a dramatist.

'While very young I extended my range and entered a Dublin that was poor and Catholic and Gaelic—a very wonderworld.' The term Catholic indicated the rebound from stalwart Protestantism, and the freedom permeating the atmosphere. Everything was of use. The vaguest thought or idea was of value. Stephens had a deep interest in what waited to be explored in every field; he was also studying the Irish language sporadically and delving in the untouched riches his country offered. Meanwhile he was twenty-nine and was ready to bring out his first important work, a book of verse.

III

The Influence of Blake

Good and bad and right and wrong!
Wave the silly words away!
This is wisdom—to be strong!
This is virtue—to be gay!
Dance

IN May 1909 *Insurrections* was issued by Maunsell & Company, who were responsible for most of the literary publications in Dublin at the time. Even when we overlook the natural weaknesses in a first volume it is difficult to realize now what an impression it must have made on Stephens's contemporaries. Colum had gone for his theme to Man and his struggle with the hostile elements, and had rejected idealized landscape; and Synge had seriously considered a method of strengthening poetry, writing: 'It may almost be said that before verse can be human again it must learn to be brutal.' But what he deemed to be brutality in his own work could appear as coarseness. His theories, too, in the preface to his poems and translations, did not appear until after *Insurrections* had been published, so that though they may have been known indirectly to Stephens, they were completely unknown to the public. Stephens was refreshing for he injected poetic idiom with a stream of vigorous down-to-earth language. With his enthusiasm for native Irish tradition he combined intuition and sympathy, and he prepared Dublin for the coming of James Larkin's labour movement. Here was a glimpse into the sordidity and the humanity of the Dublin slums. The direct attack of his stark realism and Blakean philosophy contrasted with the twilight idealism of O'Sullivan and the remoteness of Colum's country scholar.

Insurrections is a collection of songs about muddy back streets

31

and the irksome life lived under such conditions. There the sorrow of the individual must be kept private and a brave face must be shown to the world or no bread will be earned. Even the wind seems perpetually to moan. But there are moments of vision, even if people will condemn the visionary as insane, and Stephens shows that if life and fate are inexorable one can at least feel for other people. Courage, truth and kindness are aids on the way to hope; and man with the help of God and nature may attain to heaven's way of life.

The poems are more serious than in his other books. Unlike *The Hill of Vision* there are no catchy lyrics; here he was drunk with the power and music of words and on occasion, for instance in 'The Shell', he rose to magnificence of crescendo and climax. He was eager to describe the ills of the world but as yet he had not enough confidence in his over-riding philosophy to introduce a remedy so thoroughly as to leave no room for his telling pictures. 'What's the use of my abuse?' he thought.

Criticism was divided. Some critics regarded Stephens as a roguish elf who could not be judged by the standards of normal human beings, and this is the view which is current at the present day. Some were more severe and called him a naughty child. Even A.E., who had encouraged him from the beginning and had great hopes of him, said to Arnold Bax:

> I think Stephens is a little too free with Gawd (God). His attitude is rather like that of an African heathen towards his joss. When things are not going too well with our friend he bangs God about, and pitches him into the corner amongst the rubbish. And then an hour later, feeling some compunction at the forlorn appearance of the old fellow, he sets God up again and seeks to propitiate him with libation and sacrifice.[1]

Stephen Gwynn complained, when reading *Insurrections*, that Stephens reflected too many depressing experiences and not enough of what thrilled him. But, in fact, Stephens's sense of humour prevented him from dwelling too long on unhappiness, and his humanity, his most lovable characteristic, tended to make him regard the human predicament less than seriously because he knew too well, and at first hand, the horrors of

[1] *Farewell My Youth*, by Arnold Bax (1943), pp. 96–97.

poverty. In 'Righteous Anger', in the later *Reincarnations*, his rage was not sustained beyond the poem as in Synge and W. H. Davies. The poem is a burst of anger which cleans the air and leaves one free to laugh again. And in all of his satires, with the exception of 'The Gombeen Man', which is quite bitter, he was usually more amused than annoyed.

Despite their disapprobation Gwynn and others were sure that Stephens held a permanent position in Anglo-Irish literature; and it became obvious that the poet was not merely contented to shock the public into a new attitude of mind; he set out, through a number of years, to cultivate a new diction for himself which, in common with the later Irish poets, preserved all the poetry life had to offer, while affecting a more realistic medium than the poets of the Celtic Twilight had used.

He had read widely in English Literature before *Insurrections* came out, and in it, and in *The Hill of Vision*, three years later, to an even greater extent, we hear phrases taken straight from Keats, Wordsworth and Milton; the latter was resorted to as late as *Kings and the Moon* whenever Stephens's tendency was to be pretentious. But by far the strongest influences on the young Stephens, and those who contributed most to the moulding of his style and content, were Blake and Browning. Stephens was indebted to Blake both in prose and verse, and Blake was his authority for esoteric ideas; and, while his influence may have damaged Stephens's verse permanently in the later period, the typical simplicity of utterance helped Stephens to avoid Edwardian 'preciousness' and guided his method into what he considered purer phrasing and into stressing the single word or syllable. Browning served as master of his conversational tone, interesting him in experiments in metre, and teaching him how to describe the people he loved to notice. 'The Stranger', in 1907, is the first verse to employ one of Browning's individual metres and there were in *Sinn Féin* several poems on the husband and wife relationship which owe something to Browning. The different strains these poets brought out in Stephens remained at opposite poles for years, and then blended together in the style first seen in 'The Goat Paths', where the attraction of natural things and the call of mysticism display themselves.

Stephens started his career with two important qualities. The first was his insistence on what he called 'chiselling his statue'. 'If you succeed in dodging hard work in verse, well, you have also succeeded in dodging poetry,' he said in one of his late broadcasts. (This, of course, was the hard work employed after initial divine inspiration.) He was not ashamed to admit his tutors in poetry and realized these must be digested and exploited to their full before being rejected. The second was his wide vocabulary which was based upon his own vivid and personal experience. With these to his advantage, he began to experiment in metre; but the rare examples of Blake's versification—it only appears in a few poems that might have been written by Blake himself—remind us that Stephens was aware of Blake's carelessness, and that this was an instance of a poet who did not 'chisel his statue'. He preferred the forms of Spenser and Donne and Keats to those of Blake, and Browning's metres were attempted frequently in his early work, as for instance that of 'Love Among the Ruins' in 'Fifty Pounds a Year and a Pension'. It is noticeable that the choice of words in his *Seumas Beg* poems, written chiefly in 1910 and 1911, are the same as in his most characteristic poems, unlike other writers of children's poems, who assume a semi-poetic, quasi-childlike expression; and the earliest versions, though written before his son could speak, and before he was born, for Stephens was the first Seumas Beg, sound as if his son had excitedly poured out the stories while Stephens seized a pen and jotted them down at once. They are quite matter-of-fact and conversational.

James Naoise, Stephens's only son, was born on 26 October, 1909, and was named James after his father and Naoise in preparation for when the Irish language would be restored to rightful prominence. Three weeks before his son's birth Stephens stated his basic beliefs even more religiously than he had done in 'Poetry' in an article in *Sinn Féin*. 'Imagination', however, is unimpressive and has nothing new to say. He recommended the gift to businessmen and citizens as well as to artists because, he wrote, far from being a flighty or sensational attribute as is too often implied, it is rooted in real experience, stimulated by knowledge acquired, and soars to vision and prophecy. He described it as the interpreter which resolves theory to certainty; but the interesting statement in the article is his assertion that Imagination's greatest result is to be found in poetry, 'and great poetry is the highest, and indeed the most laborious work upon which the mind of man can be turned'.

His reverence for Imagination coloured his political attitude, but even more so did the tenets he adopted from William Blake, as is seen in a lecture to the Central Branch of Sinn Féin, the following year, 'Irish Idiosyncrasies'. Stephens had already gained some courage when proposing a vote of thanks after a speech by the O'Rahilly, but he remained highly nervous of public speaking until the end of his life, describing the latter occasion to John Brennan, when they were alone, with customary amusement. His throat was dry, his hands were shaking and he even refused a cigarette. An offer of some chewing-gum was accepted gratefully. When it came to his moment for speaking he put the gum into the palm of his hand, and while he talked he automatically worked it all over his hands until it formed a kind of skin. Afterwards, when he returned home, he was up half the night trying to remove the gum with any cleaning substance on which he could lay his hands, and nothing would remove it until he thought of Vim.

Stephens wished to be detached from the active political movement, perhaps through consciousness of his own physical limitations; but certainly the idealism noticeable in his early articles contributed to his pacifist tendencies. His 'Epithalamium', written at an evening's notice ('I did not then know if an epithalamium was a vegetable or a fish'), for Griffith's forthcoming wedding, is in classical vein, a product of the professional poet. Mrs. Griffith saw him only three times at Sinn Féin meetings in Griffith's house, and he seemed subdued and very much in the background. (She remembered him for his striking face, his kind dark eyes and the hair 'scattered' over his head.) In 'Irish Idiosyncrasies', Stephens referred his audience to Arthur Griffith for an enlightened viewpoint on the trend of political events. The discourse touches on prevalent characteristics hardly conducive to progress, pointing out at the same time that there must be a reprehensible element in every nation if any progress is to be achieved. 'The vices of a man or nation are often a surer index to their qualities than their virtues are,' he said. 'Good is sometimes only a negative or passive quality, an absence from evil. Evil is almost always a positive, energetic, and passionate life movement.' Energy was what he advocated in opposition to the lethargy which was reigning; even dancing was indulged in rigidly, which distressed him, for dancing should involve every part of one's body. Even one's ears should waggle. '. . . All life and all greatness comes back to that word—Energy. Genius is energy controlled definitely. Beauty is energy in form, swift curves, strong lines. Good and Evil are energies working in opposite directions.'

Wise tolerance was what he advocated, and a nation of 'strong pessimists'. The comfortable happy optimist achieves nothing. It was at this meeting that he stated clearly that his political interests were personal and of no public import: 'My business is not to direct the destinies of any nation—I wouldn't be bothered doing it if I could—but to tell stories and write verses.'

This lecture is so steeped in Blake that perhaps we should pause for a moment and consider in some detail the influence of Blake, direct and indirect, on the young writer.

Stephens was not the first of the Irish poets to be drawn towards William Blake. Enthusiasm for the poet was general in the last part of the nineteenth century. Yeats and his fellows, when reacting from the narrowness of Irish Protestantism, and interesting themselves in Theosophy, found that Blake, a literary man, had much in common with the fundamental principles of the Theosophical movement, and that he believed in the unity of things, and in the quality of life in all things. In 1893, Yeats and Ellis produced the first complete collection of Blake's works, a massive edition, in which they analyzed Blake's philosophy and included black-and-white copies of the illustrated Prophetic Books.[1] *Vala* was published for the first time. Blake's ideals, and his conviction that the poet's profession was religiously significant, were a source of inspiration to the Irish writers.

Stephens's devotion to Blake's work was more lasting than that of the other writers, and in many ways it was akin to discipleship. His first article owed to Blake was 'Imagination' published in *Sinn Féin* on 16 October 1909 and one of his last dealt with Blake exclusively—'The Purest Poet of Them All'.[2] He quoted and referred to him constantly all his life.

He began the close study of his poetry early, and at the end

[1] Stephens would have known this edition.
[2] 'The Purest Poet of Them All' (*Listener*), 6 September 1945.

of his life, though fully aware that Blake 'committed every artistic crime in the calendar', and that three-quarters of Blake's poems are merely drafts for poems, for Blake 'would not live with them'; and though he said 'I don't think I know any poem of Blake's that is perfect', and acknowledged that the difficulty about Blake is that 'he was not a serious poet, he was not a serious painter, he was not a serious philosopher, he was not quite a serious religious', Stephens still insisted:

> He is the genius, and there is no one like him, and he is the beloved, and there is no one better worth loving.[1]

Blake and Stephens had much in common. Their vision of the infinite was clearly outlined, without any of the dreaminess of A.E., or the early Yeats, and in both cases it was influenced by their love and concern for humanity. Both used a straightforward, sometimes naïve versification and had a habit of stating their beliefs in aphorisms, as A.E. had, which made them appear dogmatic. Blake's prophetic 'chanting' must have had some influence on Stephens, though it was natural to him already, and formed part of the mutual feeling which drew him to the older poet.

As well as this, the two men had an instinctive understanding of a child's mind. Blake had an idealized picture of childhood and wished all to go back to those days of vision when life was simple and based on love. There are instances of his direct influence in some of Stephens's work. In general, however, Stephens's child-poems are written from a child's point of view, a child who finds life exciting but fearful: the adult knows that experience will remove the horrors that ignorance invents. In this context 'Westland Row' may be compared to 'Holy Thursday' in *Songs of Innocence*. Occasionally childhood is idealized, more in the tradition of Robert Louis Stevenson, but, even then, the poems are a revelation of the little boy in Stephens himself calling out for pure joy, and do not picture the imagined delight of some hypothetical infant.

Both poets mourned the advance of civilization: Blake with his chimney-sweep, doomed to work among those 'dark Satanic mills', or the oppressive wheels and furnaces in *Jerusalem*; and Stephens, standing between a car and a tram, praising the stars.

[1] See footnote [2] on p. 36.

For Blake, civilization was a symbol of the Fall of Man and his preoccupation with worldly matters. But Stephens saw that it tried to oust Nature—to him the most powerful and living thing:

> There are no longer any meadows in the world . . . They came in the night and took away the green meadows, and the horses do not know what to do . . .

he prophesied in *Here Are Ladies*. However, like Blake, who in the end of *Jerusalem* saw the union of all living things once again, he foresaw a happier time:

> Horse! Horse! little horse! . . . You do not believe me. There are those who have no whips. There are children who would love to lift you in their arms and stroke your head.

Stephens also resembled Blake in his bitter attack on conventional Christianity, for he believed that it had taken away all of spontaneity and imagination from mankind. He examined Blake's theology in 'The Wisdom of the West', an article in the *Irish Review* in 1912:

> Blake does not postulate a Trinity but a quaternity, in his Republic. His battlefield is the human body; the protagonists under the titles of Urizen, Luvah, Tharmas and Urthona, are Powers, Intellect, Love, Spirit and Matter, and each of these had further its female, its emanation, its spectre, metal, space, and physical function. The inter-action and aloofness, the tyrannies, slaveries and rebellions of these are the theme. At some time one of these states is in the dominant, and again a different one takes the sway, and the battle cannot be ended until Imagination, or the Redeemer, has fused them into the peace of Universal Brotherhood, which is his objective. He postulates two golden ages; one in the beginning when each of these states was separate and untroubled by the others, and the second golden age of brotherhood and reconciliation.

The god of orthodox religion is Urizen, Reason, the manifestation of only one of God's qualities; and, at the beginning of his career, in 'Optimist', Stephens stated that he had no faith in Him. His 'Insurrection' was against this God, who is in fact the creation of mankind.

'God becomes as we are, that we may be as he,' wrote Blake. For mankind, this creation of a rational God is the easy way out of an uncomfortable relationship with a God whose demands are too exacting. But Stephens pointed out, in 'Irony', in *Songs From the Clay*, that it is difficult to respect the false God, and the man who denies the existence of God altogether places his life in danger, as the true God, to whom mankind has blinded itself, may suddenly take part in the workings of the world and revenge himself. In *The Demi-Gods*, Stephens satirized the 'created' God and the dogma of orthodox Christianity:

> 'You must repent of your own free will,' said Cuchulain, marching to the door.
>
> 'And you'd better hurry up, too,' said the other fellow, 'or I'll hammer the head of you.'

O'Brien causes chaos in heaven when, though sentenced to everlasting torment, he insists on justice for the theft of his threepenny piece. Steps are taken to settle the matter:

> A proclamation was sent through all the wards of Paradise, calling on whatever person, archangel, seraph, cherub, or accolyte, had found a threepenny piece since midday on the 10th August then instant, that the same deliver the said threepenny piece to Rhadamanthus at his court and should receive in return a free pardon and a receipt.

The good, 'even when their bliss was sealed, and their steps set on an easy path, went faltering and not daring to look round again, their ears strained to catch a "Halt, miscreant! this other is your way!" '

The tramp in *Songs From the Clay* dreams that this God of 'Justice' is faced by his own inadequacy on the Day of Judgement and forced to flee. His angels are the creatures of *The Marriage of Heaven and Hell* who 'have the vanity to speak of themselves as 'the only wise'.

> With lilting wings and eyes of holy dread,
> And curving ears strained for the great foot-fall
> And not a thought of sin . . .

A.E. also felt that they could not be pure as a result of 'systematic reasoning', but should struggle within themselves to become free from sin.

'Systematic reasoning' is what has produced Urizen, the

god of 'the philosophy of five senses'. Stephens wrote in *The Crock of Gold*:

> One of the great troubles of life is that Reason has taken charge of the administration of Justice, and by mere identification it has achieved the crown and sceptre of its master. But the imperceptible usurpation was recorded, and discriminating minds understand the chasm which still divides the pretender Law from the exiled King. In a like manner, and with feigned humility, the Cold Demon advanced to serve Religion, and by guile and violence usurped her throne; but the pure in heart still fly from the spectre Theology to dance in ecstasy before the starry and eternal goddess.

It is the unenlightened man who has made a 'Crown of Thorns' for his brow:

> He has triumphed over sin,
> He named it honour and renown,
> And thereof he made a crown of thorns.

This is Blake's 'Self enjoyings of self denial'.

Even in *The Insurrection in Dublin* in 1916 Stephens proclaimed the philosophy he shared with Blake:

> After a certain point I dislike and despise Justice. It is an attribute of God, and is adequately managed by Him alone; but between man and man no other ethics save that of kindness can give results.

Like Blake, he condemned states of sin, but not individual sinners; and he attacked human law consistently in the person of policemen. The big policeman in *The Charwoman's Daughter* is shown to be blown up with self-love. 'The Merry Policeman' has a job in hell to keep him hot, while the Philosopher in *The Crock of Gold* denies any use for policemen in the world; 'If policemen were necessary to a civilization crows would most certainly have evolved them.'

But living in this world, the Philosopher is subject to their power. Quite wrongly, he is accused of his brother Philosopher's murder and put in prison: 'When the morning came the Philosopher was taken to a car to the big city in order that he might be put on his trial and hanged. It was the custom.'

Many people find security in the conventional judicial system.

Blake saw law, not as an external force but as the constraint which mankind itself desires. 'For man has closed himself up, till he sees all things thro' narrow chinks of his cavern.' James Stephens, as Blake himself, was horrified that any arbitrary limitations might be put on the mind. His children in 'The Cage' do not understand, but instinctively sense the evil of such practice; and the Philosopher, who has reached freedom of spirit and love of his fellowmen, shudders when going into prison again:

> He strove desperately to regain his intellectual freedom, but he could not. He could conjure up no visions but those of fear. The creatures of the dark invaded him, fantastic terrors were thronging on every side: they came from the darkness into his eyes and beyond into himself, so that his mind as well as his fancy was captured, and he knew he was, indeed, in gaol.

Stephens believed one must submit to the law in body but not in spirit; for the day would come when he would be able to assert truth where Urizen has whispered lies. He and Blake were sure that the whole system of moral principles is false. Priests teach us to fight sin and stamp out evil; but this is a negative attitude to religion.

'They have conceived virtue as a repression', says Pan to the Philosopher. In *The Demi-Gods*, Patsy MacCann and the angels live outside the 'denominations' of virtue and vice, and indeed the angels are happy enough to think that all human beings do, knowing only Patsy and his tinker friends. Patsy could have said that the religious 'were rooted in their houses, and that they had no idea of life other than the trees might have which snuff for ever the same atmosphere and look on the same horizon until they droop again to the clay they lifted from.' Pan counsels Caitilin to forget the words right and wrong and to live '—as happy as the beasts'.

If we are to talk about Good and Evil, we must be careful what our attitude to them is, says Stephens. In fact evil may have some use. 'The Young-Young Man' fears lest misery and grief:

> Like misers hide a joy beyond belief.

while 'The Dodder Bank' states that God may find sin useful

when goodness is absent. Stephens himself shelters both love and hate in case he finds:

> When it's too late
> That the other was best.

Blake's central doctrine, 'Without contraries is no progression', was prominent in Stephens's early work.

> Attraction and Repulsion, Reason and Energy, Love and Hate, are necessary to Human Existence.
> From these contraries spring what the religious call Good and Evil. Good is the passive that obeys Reason. Evil is the action springing from Energy,

he wrote in *The Marriage of Heaven and Hell*. Stephens believed that we are influenced by the struggle between contraries from our birth. In the poem in *The Hill of Vision*, which he at one time regarded as his finest poem, Eve came into being from 'The House of Life and Death'. Death, as well as Life, he thought, is necessary to Man—'the Immortals are tired and cannot die'. Man may be horrified to find out that devils are blood-brothers of the Gods and fear that we have been betrayed; but in fact, the relationship could be fruitful. Blake has shown in *The Marriage of Heaven and Hell* that it is the Devil who brings the Angel to salvation through preaching the true doctrine of love to our fellows. In *The Charwoman's Daughter* Stephens stated that evil was necessary to prevent our falling into lethargy. Even a policeman has chaos in his soul and may work his way to salvation; for when we have fought our battle we will reach God:

> Your love and hate, your peace and strife . . .
> All further on the trend of life,
> And help ye still to rise.

As early as *Insurrections*, Stephens saw that in evolution lies our hope of deliverance. In *The Hill of Vision* he examined it in connection with the doctrine of reincarnation, picturing all live things coming to the Source of Life for refreshment before they set out again.[1] He also believed that it is only in the Bondage that we may prepare ourselves to return again to the Liberty,

[1] However, even in the days when he read little other than Eastern philosophy, Stephens never went deeply into the question of reincarnation.

'comprehending all things and fitted for that fiery enjoyment'. The strife of contrary influences within us is essential to this spiritual development. The power of contraries reacts on us from outside, too, for the scowl of an enemy is equally helpful in our growth. Stephens said that good is the natural outcome of evil. Evil is an active force. It is vice which we must abhor. Vice and holiness are the stagnant extremes of evil and good, and defy progress.

Stephens was convinced that all extremes in themselves are unproductive, and stated that they must meet if they are to be fertile. Even Wisdom and Love, the cardinal virtues, must join together to be fruitful. Right and wrong become inseparable for the Philosopher as he is more and more inspired by the Divine Imagination, and when these opposites merge there is perfection and finality; because, in the nature of things, when the striving of contraries ceases:

> there is chime
> At last where discord was.

God will be united with Satan, in that happy time; the Devil seated beside 'one who has been crucified'.

If contraries are to cause progression, they must in themselves move, alive, full of energy. So it is not surprising that Stephens was wholehearted in his support of Blake's formula: 'Energy is Eternal Delight'. As we have seen in his early propaganda for Ireland, Stephens called for a policy of energy, motivated by the conflict of good and evil. This was the only attitude which might cause improvement, and bring about a healthy atmosphere in the country.

The Philosopher's maxims are all based on energy, and it is the refusal to grow stagnant that wins salvation for the surviving one. Mary Makebelieve, 'to do that which is pleasing to the gods', goes forward. 'The Imp', endeavouring to worship the god of 'Yea and Nay', gives up, protesting: 'Lust of life shall make me sin'. In *The Demi-Gods* too Stephens insisted on 'a well-packed head and energy—that is the baggage for life, it is the baggage for eternity'.

Energy throbs through all things; if it is not in men, so much the worse for them, for it sings in the stones. In 1930 Stephens wrote in *Forum* that jazz had a great future because of its ceaseless energy. The Philosopher in 'The Tavern in the Town' states that 'if we are wildly and ecstatically joyous then we will become creators'. Joy of life moves the frog 'to almost ceaseless activity', but 'Policemen and puckauns, and advertising agents, and fish, do not dance at all, and this is because they have hard hearts'. False intellectual pride must be abandoned for a dance of gaiety and then we will cease to be miserable and suspicious, and become fearless and companionable to all creatures.

Stephens poured Blake's fundamental doctrine of love and joy through his whole work. Yeats believed in it too:

> For the good are always the merry,
> Save by an evil chance,
> And the merry love to fiddle,
> And the merry love to dance.

But to Stephens it was far more important than to Yeats. Yeats looked on joy as a blessed condition where one is unaware of sin; but even then he was chiefly occupied with the question of its reality. In Stephens it resembled the 'Infant Joy' of *Songs of Innocence*:

A Leprechaun is of more value to the Earth than is a Prime Minister or a stockbroker, because a Leprechaun dances and makes merry.

he wrote in *The Crock of Gold*, and he also stated that 'Laughter is linked with holiness', and 'Dancing is the first and last duty of man.' With Oothoon, in 'The Visions of the Daughters of Albion', he advanced beyond Theotormon's adherence to the word of the Law and would sing:

Love! Love! Love! happy happy Love! free as the mountain wind!

Stephens allowed joy to overwhelm him and even when joy acquired a mystic flavour it had nothing to do with magic. In this he differed from A.E. and Yeats, who saw a 'wizard glow' in the night, or looked on Nature as a necromancer. Stephens also rejected the magic in religion which appealed to the other poets, and made fun of Brien O'Brien, the serious minded magician, in *The Demi-Gods*. His imagery is filled with a love of humanity, as is that of Blake. The centaurs stamp with 'fierce glee' and wheel around in 'furious brotherhood', like

Los, in *Jerusalem*, who 'rag'd and stamp'd the earth in his might and terrible wrath'. Nature sometimes enjoys an even more blessed state than humans. With Blake, who chanted to all who might hear him, 'Everything that lives is Holy,' James Stephens defied orthodox religion and, swept into Communion with Nature, cried:

There is no Sin.

In *The Crock of Gold* Stephens was to attempt a full exposition of Blake's philosophy; before he had referred to it only where he required support for beliefs. Meanwhile his energies were still directed towards writing for *Sinn Féin*, and he also published some broadsides with the Cuala Press. Early in 1911 he was on the committee of *The Irish Review*, writing to friends for subscriptions and helping to prepare a prospectus.

The Irish Review was founded by George Houston, a professor in the College of Science, who was prominent in Dublin literary circles. He was an extrovert, inclined to burn up with sudden enthusiasm for new projects; it was very suddenly that he proposed to launch a new magazine, and he had the name decided upon before the plans were even on paper.

Immediately Stephens, Thomas MacDonagh, Pádraic Colum and Mary Colum were gathering at Houston's house in the Dublin hills for discussions about it. Miss Alderton (Houston's housekeeper) called it 'The Bogey Book', because they referred to it as the dummy. Houston outlined his aim. *The Irish Review* was to be a literary journal, published monthly, which should report current political and economic developments in its editorial notes. Each month it should contain, besides the literary articles, a reproduction, perhaps in colour, of a famous painting.

Houston wanted an article on Synge for the first issue and Mary Colum wrote this. John Eglinton did many articles on books, and Pádraic Colum wrote the editorial notes, having been advised to talk them over with Pádraic Pearse, then headmaster of St. Enda's School. Thomas MacDonagh, the poet, who was chief assistant in Pearse's school, would have been an obvious choice as literary editor; he was at the time preparing a criticism of Elizabethan poetic technique, and he lived quite near Houston, in the gate-lodge of his house; but Houston trusted *The Irish Review* to Colum, since he feared the political influence on MacDonagh of Joseph Plunkett, and indeed his fears were latterly justified. Houston was of northern birth and he hated Plunkett's mystic Catholicism. Pearse's dedication, on the other hand, impressed Houston; Pearse, of course, believed that 'nationality is a spirituality', but whether he faced the problems of education or of his country's politics, he based his high-flown idealist principles on concrete plans, and took well-considered, determined action, and Houston felt nothing but admiration for his newly-founded school where the boys were encouraged to be original and independent. Houston also had a great opinion of A.E. and supported his dictum that now was the time for communal expression and for building a new Ireland with communal effort, and these were the ideals *The Irish Review* was to develop. Houston already had experience of publishing from his own paper *Irish Gardens*, to which he was devoted and in which Helen Curran and Pádraic Colum were writing. *Irish Gardens* and *The Irish Review* were printed by Maneko, a Jew who ran the Irish Society. Lord Dunsany contributed funds for a short period.

The first issue of *The Irish Review* appeared in March 1911. For the first few months it was produced with immense enthusiasm. Houston, though nominally the editor, hardly ever wrote anything and he gradually drifted away. Pádraic Colum became his successor as editor in March 1912. Colum, Mac-Donagh and Stephens took it in turns to prepare each issue and all wrote in it and acquired articles from fellow writers.

The serial 'Mary, Mary', known at the time as 'Mary Makebelieve', or, since Stephens was becoming interested in the Irish language, 'Mary Macbelieve', was most popular and held the paper together.[1] When it was published in book form in 1912 the title was changed to *The Charwoman's Daughter*, and it is the only one of Stephens's books which might be called a novel. *The Charwoman's Daughter* is a story of life in the tenements of Dublin. Mrs. Makebelieve is a charwoman who would like to bring her daughter up to be equipped for a life of leisure, married to a handsome man of fortune. Mary is now sixteen

---

[1] It is said that when he offered it to the paper Professor Houston had to go through the manuscript and correct the spelling and formation of the story.

and has not yet had to go to work, and she spends the days, while her mother is out, wandering about the streets of Dublin, feeding her imagination on all she sees about her. These pictures delighted Stephens's contemporaries who saw George Moore in the tiredest man in the world, who gazes at everyone as if seeing those who are dead but whom he does not regret; Yeats in the thin black young man who buzzes like a bee; A.E. in the picture of the big man with the brown beard; and Synge in the unkempt man with a pale face and drooping moustache. One day Mary meets the big policeman and she realizes that she is a child no more. A delightful vignette of a young girl and her growing experience of life, the novel in fact describes some of the seamier side of living and an attempt at abduction; but the whole air of the book is innocent and like a fairytale. Stephens advocated adherence to the religion of love and worship of the God Freedom. Mary's thoughts may be uncertain and confused but her mother believes firmly in a pattern of life which directs one's path.

> In most of the trouble in life she divined men and women not knowing or not doing their duty, which was to love one another and to be neighbourly and obliging to their fellows. A partner, a home and children—through the loyal co-operation of these she saw happiness, and, dimly, a design of so vast an architecture as scarcely to be discussed.

A publisher in Boston, Edward O'Brien, offered Stephens £100 for the story and this financial success encouraged him to continue with *The Crock of Gold* and form it into a novel.

After its initial impact, the need for a publication of such idealism seemed to die out and it became harder and harder to find the money to print *The Irish Review* (they charged only sixpence a copy) and to find contributors. A change too came over the founders of the paper. The original atmosphere of youthful enthusiasm channelled by the shrewd northerner and characterized by mature accomplished work altered as they observed with irritation that Yeats was detaching himself from politics and devoting himself to his career as a writer.

Everyone had been occupied with outside ventures which they had brought to the paper and recorded there. Stephens alone had imported nothing and simply contributed his personal talent. His concerns outside *The Irish Review* were the hardship of those living in the slums and the optimistic course of events leading up to the Strike, and he studied the work of English writers rather than what was happening at home. Now the outside interests of the other writers were the death of the original magazine. The Home Rule Bill overshadowed every consideration and Pearse was abandoning his pacifist views for a militant policy. In June 1913 MacDonagh and Plunkett bought *The Irish Review* from Houston to produce it as a volunteer magazine. After this it ceased to be a literary paper and the preoccupation with political and social questions caused a falling-off of intellectual stock. It appeared only twice more.

Stephens's interest in the social and political advance of his time did not cease and he was to publish articles in *The Irish Worker* and *The Irish Citizen*, but literary work was becoming the main concern for him ever since the day when he raced in excitedly to Dr. Solomons waving the cheque for £100 from America for *The Charwoman's Daughter*. He had never seen such a large cheque before and since all of the Irish writers found their dealings with Maunsell somewhat difficult he was encouraged by the thought of a new publisher. He had offers too from literary agents. On 1 April 1912 he rejected an offer from James B. Pinker of Talbot House, London, to act as his literary agent and a few days later he refused Pinker's offer for help in publishing occasional work. He had made up his mind long ago, he said, to produce no occasional work unless it was specially commissioned. However, on 19 April, he wrote accepting Pinker as his agent and he told him that he wanted to remain with one publisher alone and this was Macmillan. *The Hill of Vision* had been published in New York in February, and later by Maunsell of Dublin, but when *The Charwoman's Daughter* appeared a short time later the change-over had been completed, and this was largely due to Pinker. Stephens sent him the final manuscript of *The Crock of Gold* in July 1912 asking that it should not have the same salmon-pink cover on it as Macmillan had put on *The Charwoman's Daughter*, and he suggested changing the title to 'The Thin, Thin Woman's Husband', but after discussion the original title was, perhaps fortunately for him, retained.

The Hill of Vision, as its name indicates, was written on an elevated plane. The whole tenor of the work is lighter than that of *Insurrections;* when a mood of gloom struck him all was not hopeless, and the many poems about human relationship have a gentler air. Consciously a poet, he first summoned the Muse, making it plain that he wished to disperse the conventionally termed 'good' and 'bad' by spreading laughter and gaiety. He would fly into the sky and abandon all the dull preoccupations which weigh down his wings. He referred constantly to Christian imagery throughout, though usually with a humorous bent, and in particular in his description of the Fall where fallen man is but a jackanapes full of fun; but behind the lyrical verse is a deep adherence to Blake's tenets. 'The Fairy Boy' might have been written by Blake. Even more striking is 'Mount Derision' which is directly borrowed. At the end of 'The Visions of the Daughters of Albion' there is an engraving of Theotormon and Oothoon chained to each other, striving to free themselves, but inextricably bound. Stephens must have seen this picture, reproduced in Yeats and Ellis's edition of Blake's collected works, for in *The Hill of Vision* he seated this couple on Mount Derision and showed how Thought and Heart originally worked peaceably together, like brother and sister, until desire and strife chained them in matrimony and hate crept in; and now they must suffer

> till they see
> Love is crowned by Liberty.

However, the debt to Blake is even more apparent in *The Crock of Gold*, his most famous book. *The Crock of Gold* appeared in October 1912. It was immediately popular and a best-seller of its day, and since 1912 has gone into countless editions. Stephens never regarded it as his best book; he believed that *The Charwoman's Daughter* (a book not involved with such an immense proposition) was his finest work in prose; but *The Crock of Gold* is important in that it contains the basis of his somewhat confused philosophy and owes a considerable debt to William Blake. *The Crock of Gold*, indeed, is an accumulation of previous work bound together by a symbolic plot. The children and their games came from observation at home, and the Philosopher and his monologues, and two of the short stories, come from *Sinn Féin*.

In the beginning of *Jerusalem*, God calls man but is spurned; and Stephens, too, as Yeats in 'Into the Twilight', felt God's

49

loneliness and need for the companionship of man. 'Oh Thou un-happy God,' says Satan, seeing His powerlessness. For the true God has been divided through the birth of self-hood, and it is necessary that His parts be rejoined before He is complete, and man without sin any more. 'The world has forgotten me,' Angus Og laments:

> I am the desolate god forbidden to utter my happy laughter . . .
> who will deliver me from Thought, from the base holiness of
> Intellect, the maker of chains and traps?

Blake lamented this state of affairs, in *Jerusalem*, where he denounced 'abstract Philosophy warring in enmity against Imagination'. This is the theme of *The Crock of Gold*. Stephens approved of Blake as a myth-maker in modern literature, and sought to work out Blake's philosophy in his novel, also using a myth, but making the terms suitable for people of today. The two philosophers in *The Crock of Gold* have dedicated their lives to the acquisition of knowledge; and it is only the intuition of one that makes him resist death, and leads him to investigate the possibility that the ultimate end may be 'gaiety and music and a dance of joy'. Through his meeting with Pan, the god of woods and pastures, his eyes are opened to the beauty of nature, and he throws away 'petty' thought in favour of 'motion and emotion'. The three groups of people he meets after seeing Pan are also directed by instinct, and there is a touch of sadness in each of them: this is because they are manifestations of man living naturally, abandoned by the divine spark. The Philoso-pher reaches Pan when his senses are revived, for he has seen Caitilin naked. But he comes to Angus Og by chance, his only merit being the collapse of his former conventional opinions. Nature attends Angus Og also, instinct is a part of him, but the essential spirit in him is Los—The Divine Imagination—which heightens his natural powers. Both gods are manifestations of the Eternal Will—Blake's impersonal Immortal Will—but while Pan is supported by Earth, Angus Og enjoys the protec-tion of air. Man has to choose which he wants.

'Lo, I am sealed in the caves of nonentity,' says Angus Og.

Until Man, who is Thought, mates with woman, who is Intuition and Emotion, and their powers of head and heart are exchanged, they will be alone, self-centred, and needing the link of Divine Imagination. Stephens still believed this in *The Insurrection in Dublin* where he described imagination as 'intelligent kindness'. Caitilin, who went to Pan because of physical love, chooses Angus Og because his need of her is very great—an example of Blake's woman's Pity, and part of the purification through self-forgetfulness necessary for salvation. The Philosopher returns to his wife, now filled with divine love and cleansed from his former selfishness. All his acquaintances after the visit to Angus Og are innocent and carefree, living only with their spirits and the Wisdom which is Love. The Philosopher greets each with an embrace, and, in this new frame of mind, gives his wife an unexpected kiss when he comes home. Divine Love demands demonstration among the angels, also, when they have to part with Patsy and Mary, at the end of *The Demi-Gods*.

The Thin Woman, who represents intuition, has had to 'be purified by the performance of that sacrifice which is called the Forgiveness of Enemies', for according to Blake, 'Without Forgiveness of Sin, Love is Itself Eternal death'; and the rite takes place in the presence of the Sun and wind, the natural powers. She is then approached by the three Absolutes, each with a terrible extreme, but realizes that they are not in themselves separately the full aspect of God.

'Annihilate the selfhood in me; be thou all my life!' cried Blake in *Jerusalem*. Like the Philosopher and Caitilin in their state of salvation, the Thin Woman has learnt that 'the duty of life is the sacrifice of self; it is to renounce the little ego that the mighty ego may be freed'. Realization of the doctrine of annihilation of self alone brings Happiness, the State where 'the knowledge of man is added to the gaiety of a child'. The Philosopher represents the first of these components, Caitilin the second; and both achieve union with their opposite, and their new power helps them to rescue the intellect of Man from his prison. Though selfhood is repudiated, Stephens shared Blake's horror of the loss of individuality and stressed that 'they moved freely each in his personal whim, and they moved also with the unity of one being', which reminds us of Christian unity in Christ.

James Stephens never definitely stated his belief in Blake's doctrine that 'Man has no body distinct from his Soul', but his attitude of pure enjoyment of all physical things, gaily united with the spiritual, indicates how important the things of the body were to him. Blake had at first attempted an ascetic life but later he rejected it as incompatible with his genius, and only condoned it in itself when it was prompted by the 'desire of raising other men into a perception of the infinite'. The Philosopher, before his conversion, fears that civilization may be destroyed by the triumph of sensualism, as he has always believed in mind above matter; yet the impact of sexual feeling brings a richness to life which he had not known before. 'Did the sunlight not stream from his head and life from his finger-tips?' This experience helps him on his road for he notices things about which he had only theorized before.

Similarly Caitilin, though she was coming fresh to God from the Age of Innocence, the Philosopher as a contrast coming with experience, had to acquaint herself with sensual love before she was fitted for the divine love of Angus Og. God Himself, in 'The Lonely God', longs for a mate and knows He will have one 'when she hath grown to Me in space serene'; for God will not be complete in Himself till every man has achieved the great ecstasy of divine communion with all things.

'I make no mountainous claim for Blake as a poet, much as I love him, but he is still (as Fuseli said of him long ago) very good to steal from; and let it be conceded that theft is the first duty of man,' Stephens was to write later; and it is true as we have seen that he borrowed various ideas and quotations directly from Blake. The Philosophers' wives base all their maxims on secrecy, reminding us of Blake's Enitharmon, who rejoices that, while she is in power, 'from her childhood shall the little female spread nets in every secret path'. Blake's belief that no one is a Christian but he who is 'A Poet, a Painter, a Musician, an Architect' is supported by Stephens in 'Hail and Farewell', in *The Hill of Vision*, and also in *The Crock of Gold*, where he speaks of the Holy Ghost as 'The Great Artist'; and, like Blake, who gives his readers 'the end of a golden string', Angus Og leads people to him with an airy thread 'reaching from his own place to wherever you are, and if he doesn't want to see you, you will never find out where he is, not if you were to walk for a year or two years'.

Most interesting of all is the point in *The Crock of Gold* where Stephens turns to the *Descriptive Catalogue* of 1809, for the original of his 'Three Absolutes'. Blake's picture of 'The Ancient Britons' is lost but a full account of it is recorded:

> In the last Battle of King Arthur, only Three Britons escaped; these were the strongest Man, the Beautifullest Man, and the Ugliest Man; these three marched through the field unsubdued, as Gods, and the Sun of Britain set, but shall rise again with tenfold splendour when Arthur shall wake from sleep and resume his dominion over earth and ocean . . .
>
> The Strong Man represents the human sublime. The Beautiful Man represents the human pathetic, which was in the wars of Eden divided into Male and female. The Ugly Man represents the human reason. They were originally one man, who was fourfold; he was self-divided, and his real humanity slain on the stems of generation, and the form of the fourth was like the Son of God. How he became divided is a subject of great sublimity and pathos.

Stephens's characters are 'quite naked', like Blake's *Ancient Britons*.

> The Beauty proper for sublime art is lineaments or forms and features that are capable of being the receptacles of intellect . . .
> The face and limbs that deviates or alters least, from infancy to old age, is the face and limbs of greatest Beauty and perfection,

wrote Blake. And so the Most Beautiful Man of *The Crock of Gold* is 'of mighty stature, and yet so nobly proportioned, so exquisitely slender and graceful', that there is 'no idea of gravity or bulk'. His face is 'kingly and youthful and of a terrifying serenity'. Blake's Strong Man is considered a 'receptacle for Wisdom' and is compact, for 'Strength consists in accumulation of power to the principal seat' and not in extent or bulk; whereas, in Stephens the Strong Man is 'so broad . . . that his great height seemed diminished'. It is in the case of the Ugly Man that Stephens differs most from Blake, for, while both believe he is repulsive, Stephens prefers to think that Ugliness has a 'horrible intelligence', and, for Blake true Ugliness is the 'incapability of Intellect'. With both poets, however, the Three Absolutes remain for ever unsubdued, for to them 'in the eternal order come all the peoples of the world to be regenerated for ever'. Everyone desires them and they desire everybody—'it is not lawful, even for the Absolute, to outgrow Desire'; and they are only subject to Him 'who liveth in all things', Jesus Christ, the one person who does not desire them.

Stephens again departs from his original when interpreting the Absolutes:

> Beauty is Thought, and Strength is Love, and Ugliness is Generation. The home of Beauty is the head of man, the home of Strength is the heart of man, and in the loins Ugliness keeps his dreadful state.

The allocating of their situations can be traced to *The Marriage of Heaven and Hell* where Blake calls 'the head sublime, the heart Pathos, the genitals Beauty, the hands and feet proportion.'

Stephens refused to attribute beauty to sex in *The Crock of Gold* though he admitted its magnetic power, but he changed his mind in *The Demi-Gods*, where it is the beautiful archangel Art who represents Generation. Blake's Britons may be named Tharmas, Luvah, and Urizen and they must be overcome by the fourth part of God, Los, the Imagination, before they can be bound together again. Each by himself is terrifying in strength. Caeltia and Finaun, two Absolutes in *The Demi-Gods*, say:

> There is nothing in the world could stand against us two; there is nothing in the world could stand against one of us.

But they lack completion until merged with their opposites in the divine breath. Like the 'hopelessly barren' hatred, in themselves the Absolutes are final, and 'finality is the greatest evil which can happen in the world of movement'. They are stagnant and sterile. This is wrong according to Blake, because excess of sorrow must laugh, excess of joy must weep. The Thin Woman rightly rejects the advances of the Three Absolutes, as she realizes that torments of the mind are necessary and cannot be exchanged for pleasures, final in themselves, without denying any hope of the Absolutes being rejoined to Los.

Stephens did not follow Blake blindly as his master, however. Though for a time he turned away from Christianity, Blake regretted this towards the end of his life and reasserted the Lamb as Redeemer. Jesus is an essential spirit in his doctrine, and, in *Jerusalem*, he acknowledges no other salvation for man except through Christ. His allegiance to Nature seems to be bound up in Christianity, too. Stephens, on the other hand, never owned Christianity as his religion. A.E., in spite of his pagan beliefs, could never abandon the imagery of Christianity; but Stephens reverted to it only when he knew his audience thought in conventional terms. His picture of the Creation and the Fall was confused, and varied greatly according to the different influences exerted on him at the times of writing. He departed from Blake when he said: 'Chaos is the first Condition.' Then, in *The Demi-Gods*, he described the Creation in Theosophical terms. In *The Charwoman's Daughter*, he had not yet shaken off orthodoxy, for he saw the origin of the Fall in the careless words of a gay young man who says 'Let Truth go to Hell.' He drew the Fall in neo-Platonic terms in 'At the Edge of the Sea'. Here man is the free river which falls from the light of day into a cave beside the sea, that is, into ignorance in the material world.

Referring to the Gospel, he echoed Christ's second coming in *The Crock of Gold* where Angus Og tells his bride,

> On a time not distant we will go to them again, and we will not return from that journey, for we will live among our people and be at peace.

God for him was Alpha and Omega—'in the genesis of life, love is at the beginning and end of things'.

In general, however, he was free of the imagery of orthodox religion. He attacked the doctrinal God in a comparatively small percentage of poems, blaming Him for being inadequate and for lack of co-operation with the world; but God to him never stopped being Nature and Love. Nature, independent of any doctrine, breathed the essence of God and was sometimes the channel by which God might be reached. As he read more and more into the realm of Eastern mysticism, towards the end of his life, Stephens's creed became less confused, and it was in Buddhism that he found the answer to his perplexities, and a satisfactory personal philosophy of life.

IV

The Influence of Blake
and of Theosophy

He had somehow discovered part of the first syllable of the
great word.

The Demi-Gods

IN 1912 Stephens decided to resign from his post in Mr.
Mecredy's office and to devote his life to writing. At last his
work was providing sufficient income and he and his family
were able to move from the tiny single-roomed flat in Mount
Street to more spacious premises in Killeen Road in Rathmines.
In addition to material improvement and to fresh acquaintance-
ships which he enjoyed and knew were beneficial, he now felt
himself honoured in coming to the notice of the austere Yeats,
who usually held himself aloof from A.E.'s protégés. Just a year
later, in November 1913, when *The Crock of Gold* was chosen as
the outstanding contemporary work and Stephens was awarded
the Edmund Polignac prize of one hundred pounds, Yeats was
most complimentary in his speech to the Royal Society of
Literature and referred to him as the most promising of the
rising Irish writers. In particular he said with delight that this
was not mere chance; Stephens had absorbed into him all that
his native city had to offer as well as any other literary influences
congenial to him and he foresaw a great future for him. He
reflected the excitement and literary discussion in Dublin as
Elizabethan dramatists had recorded the live spirit of their
age.

Yeats was to reserve his good opinion of Stephens for later he
found that he of all the Irish writers was most interested in the
system described in *A Vision*, though Stephens himself used the
symbols in his work only once; and the personal interest was

56

reciprocal, Yeats demonstrating greater control and development of the material in the theme of *The Cat and the Moon*, which Stephens outlined briefly a few years before him in *In The Land of Youth.*

Stephens never gave himself airs. He never failed to show the same kindness to other aspiring writers as A.E. had shown to him. The Gifford sisters were introduced into A.E.'s house by Robert Lind's mother-in-law, Mrs. Dryhurst, who enthusiastically renamed the girls with ancient Irish names, to A.E.'s intense gratification. On the important evening the girls came into the large room with folding doors very shyly, but their unease was quickly dispersed by Stephens, who called them over to where he was sitting, his feet high above the ground, and talked to them for the rest of the evening in his friendly nasal Dublin voice. 'Do you like dogs?' he began.—'I do. I feel I'm an honorary dog myself.' He told them of how he had met Maud Gonne (who was very tall) at one of the literary evenings and how he had had to run across the room and climb up her to speak to her.

One of the houses Stephens used to visit was the Reddins' house at Artane, and he was most friendly and encouraging to the future Justice, who was a student at the time. Kenneth Reddin met him at an exhibition of pictures in St. Stephen's Green one day and saw him staring at Darrell Figgis, with his streaky beard, and bearded Ernest Boyd. 'I'm feeling biblical,' Stephens remarked, 'I never thought I'd see them in the same room together—Jesus Christ and Judas Iscariot.' On another occasion while they were drinking coffee in Fry's café, Stephens's attention wandered and was fixed on a man coming in through the door. He was a small, timid man who walked furtively as if he had no right to be there, and hung up his coat on the rack in a secretive manner. Stephens pointed him out to Reddin and embarked on a story about a dishonest solicitor's clerk, who was awaiting indictment for embezzlement, building the tale up to a high degree of tension. He then advised Reddin to go home and write a story about it before he forgot the details of the actions.

Confident though he might appear to those whose feet were not yet on the bottom rung of the ladder, Stephens was filled with diffidence in the company of those he did not know too well, for his humility was untouched by fame. Thomas Bodkin was his closest friend at this time and with A.E. would advise him about proofs and manuscripts, and the young writer after knocking on the front door used to come straight up to his friend's room at the top of the house and eat barm brack and apples while they discussed literature together. He timidly avoided the other inmates of the house, but, later, confronted by Bodkin's younger sister Emma, and realizing she must feel even shyer than he, immediately put her at her ease by agreeing that *The Charwoman's Daughter* was his favourite book (this some time after *The Adventures of Seumus Beg* was published). Sympathy was one of his great gifts. Enthusiasm would carry him away, too, and he would relax into a fascinating monologue on occasions where he might have felt awkward. Augustus Green, the Head Librarian in the National Library, invited him to meet Lady Iredell who had very much admired *The Crock of Gold*. A.E. and Pádraic Colum were also at the party, but James Stephens held undivided attention for a great deal of the time. His stand-up collar came adrift from his shirt unnoticed and moved about his neck as he told harrowing stories of his work as a plumber's mate, then of the soap factory where the smell nearly killed him, and finally of the solicitor's office where the daily grind inspired 'Fifty Pounds a Year and a Pension'. The party moved from the dinner table to sit in a circle about the room and the conversation was monopolized by the three writers who threw words and phrases to each other, Lady Iredell remembers, 'like tennis balls'.

Like A.E., Stephens was interested in social matters and in a series of articles in *The Irish Citizen*[1] he attacked 'The Populace Mind' which stubbornly opposed the franchise for women. 'The Populace Mind' was his name for the official attitude to changes in government and law, the unenlightened view that old established ideas were best and sustained civilization. Women, he felt, were not equal to men, but totally different, and had been held back from political prominence through very inferior education. This should be rectified instantly for not only might they contribute something fresh, and provide a new slant that was alien to men, on affairs of importance, but in their hands

---

[1] 'The Populace Mind' (1 June, 8 June, 15 June, and 22 June 1912).

lies the future of man since they are so deeply concerned with his upbringing. 'Progress' was Stephens's constant chant; 'we shall fight upwards to what is Good'. In *The Irish Worker* in 1913 he called on the Irish clergy to 'Come off that fence' and support the Irish labour movement which was part of world progress and something in which to take pride. The trade union leader, James Larkin, exponent of the General strike, had clung valiantly to his desire for better working conditions; as a result he had suffered in jail and could not be bribed. Now he must be supported and clergy and workers must commit themselves wholeheartedly. He reiterated his Blakean standpoint: 'You can do nothing without fighting something'. Then he appealed to the ordinary working man, pouring out a bitter condemnation of the Roman Catholic Church, in which he identified the priests with his *bête noir*, the policeman:

> In Ireland today the Church is a lie. The attitude of the clergy throughout this dispute has been cynical and disgusting to the last degree. If they dared they would have ordered you back to your masters; they are so used to ordering in Ireland; that the difference between a priest and a policeman is too slight to talk about. They did not dare to order you back this time, so they sat on the fence.

Writers too were trounced severely in some letters to *The Irish Homestead*.[1] In February 1913, under his pseudonym James Esse, he reminded A.E. gently that the poets did not create Cuchulain, but that Cuchulain inspired poets to sing about him; and a week later he deplored the current tendency to revel in patriotism and to reach back to dead ideals; he disliked also the love of the Abbey Theatre for peasant drama. His comments were humorous, however. 'I will remove my hand,' he wrote, 'for but one moment from your pocket while I inscribe myself most lovingly—Your friend, James Esse.' 'The Sirocco', printed in October after many others had joined the controversy, was more satirical. The lethargy of the antiquarian poets who extolled chastity, religion, wit, hospitality and noble peasants, 'cutting lies into verse lengths', was compared to that of the members of parliament, who after all had been chosen by these 'gifted people'. But, Stephens said, the reactionary movement

---

[1] *The Irish Homestead*, February 1913, October 1913.

in Ulster was promising and he hoped the Volunteers[1] would liquidate the noble peasant. James Larkin alone escaped his satire. 'The entire press of Ireland has been shouting knave at him so loudly that I divine there must be good in the man,' the writer concluded. 'He says, anyhow, that he is discontented, but the poets don't.'

Stephens's own plan was to widen his literary horizons by leaving Ireland for a period. He had been reading English writers and now he decided to look at French. His move to Paris was, unfortunately, unwise in many respects, for though he had felt it would be stimulating to his intellect, and consequently spent long periods there, literary consciousness robbed him of his facility for writing. He paid his first visit to Paris in 1912. When he returned F. R. Higgins rushed to Austin Clarke in distress. 'He told me,' Austin Clarke wrote in *The Irish Times*, 'that on the evening before, as he was on his way to A.E.'s literary gathering, he had seen an extraordinary little bundle moving rapidly along the dim-lit Rathgar Avenue, and was much puzzled. When he came closer, he discovered that it was the tiny James Stephens wrapped up in an enormous French cavalry officer's cloak.' Stephens had his portrait painted in this 'candle extinguisher' cloak by Patrick Tuohy, and at first he made a practise of wearing it after dark, but when Dublin had recovered from the initial shock he did not wear it so constantly. He used to be seen marching back to his flat in Mount Street with a long roll of French bread under his arm every evening. In January 1913 he began to learn French, and after a while could read it easily though he never could speak it fluently. In his letters to Thomas Bodkin he would use French words and phrases, especially when he first returned to Paris. 'I have noted your programme of lectures as a way of learning French,' he wrote from Paris in May; 'it is admirable but just now I am told the lectures are all over . . .' In June he announced that he was taking the study of French seriously, and he wrote a month later to say, 'I go to school every morning at

[1] Sir Edward Carson's volunteers were formed in case of Home Rule to fight for reunion with England. They increased bitterness in the south since the Government did not order their disbandment even though military groups were forbidden. The Irish Volunteers were founded in retaliation in the south of Ireland.

8.30 for a hour "with shining morning face". I renew my youth. But my french is as coy as your gaelic.'

In May 1913 the Stephenses had returned to Paris to stay with Spicer Simson, the sculptor, while looking for a flat of their own, and, in June, they took a three-room flat a few doors away from Simson, at 11, Rue Campagne-Première, so that there was constant intercourse between the households.[1] The first visit lasted for two years. However, in essence, with the exception of *Here Are Ladies*, Stephens's work was unaltered by the change in surroundings, for Stephens did not mix much with the native inhabitants. Mrs. Stephens often attended Maud Gonne's Tuesday evenings with a friend, but Stephens himself remained at home, feeling diffident about his small knowledge of French. When his Dublin friends visited Paris he had their company; and he used to take Maud Gonne's son, Seán MacBride, who was at school there, for cake and ices on his exeat days, helping him sympathetically in his search for unusual stamps. But Paris increased his nationalistic feeling; and he was rather perturbed when he heard young MacBride refer to visits from Arthur Lynch, now a British army officer, in case it might influence him in the wrong direction.

He was never at ease in the flat in Rue Campagne-Première, which had an empty atmosphere. 'These concierges are strange people,' he wrote to Bodkin on 21 May:

(I mean the system is strange, but I have quite forgotten how to write). Meanwhile the beauty of this city grows more on me mixed with a certain gentle melancholy for Dublin. You know Dublin really has points, certain pleasant incompetencies. The first shattering blow my preconceptions received was that of the polite french people. They are a mighty careful, businesslike, adequate people and they do not waste any more time in being polite than we do. No one has yet been rude to me or anything like that—but somehow one has a tradition. It's shattered I'm glad to say—a race of polite people would be utterly horrible ... Language deserts me utterly when face to face with the aboriginals but my resolve holds good that when I return to Ireland I will riot among your french books ... The only thing that makes these french women and men noteworthy is their attitude of independence and self-respect.

[1] Spicer Simson later struck a medal of James Stephens.

In October 1913 Stephens published *Here Are Ladies*. These are stories written earlier in his career but they are now treated in a new way with definite French influence, the title if nothing else, with its French flavour, giving evidence of his whereabouts. He had been working at them since January when he had received the commission, in Dublin, and he had had to withdraw from a part in an Irish version of *The Schuler's Child, Mac na Mná Deirce*, because the stories would, he thought, take up every square inch of his mind and his time.[1] He had now worked over and over each sentence and phrase in his writing. The ideology of Blake, which pervaded his work before and sings in *Five New Songs*, published at the same time, and later in *Songs from the Clay* and *The Adventures of Seumas Beg*, was forgotten now for the sophistication of French models. Much of *Here Are Ladies* consists of characteristic sketches and amusing stories, first written for *Sinn Féin* when he was unknown; he now adopted an impersonal manner, deleting the names of the characters and attempting some psychological analysis. *Etched in Moonlight*, fifteen years later, is similar in spirit to *Here Are Ladies*, though even more bereft of personality and Stephens's engaging whimsy, and in both these collections of stories, inspired in Paris, his intellectual faculty choked his strong point, narrative. The more frivolous stories depend on a delightful humour and deep perception, enriched by a lightness of touch and glorious moments of fantasy, but when more serious his perception is weighed down with dullness. The description of the charming untrustworthy lodger shows him at his best:

> He came in the night-time with the stars and the moon. He was running like a youthful god, she thought, for her mind had not yet been weaned from certain vanities, and she could not see that a gigantic policeman was in his wake, tracking him with elephantine bounds, and now and again snatching a gasp from hurry to blow furious warnings on a whistle.

The policeman was always the butt of Stephens's imagination and wit.

He had decided to remain in France and, with the exception of some months at home in summer 1914, and a visit to London to receive the de Polignac prize on 28 November 1913, which

[1] Letter to Seán Ford, 21 January 1913.

he prolonged for a week so that he might see MacKenna and some other old friends, he lived in Paris for the next two years. On 7 October he wrote to Bodkin to say that he had taken a room in the Rue Boissonade where he was doing his writing and that he had finished a three-act play:

> A Strindbergian cleverality & nothing more—certainly it is not & will never be marketable. The subject is unpleasant & the treatment is no more than so so.

This must have been the beginnings of *The Demi-Gods*, which was written first as a play and in the opening scene in particular has a dramatic directness, far more dramatic, indeed, than *The Marriage of Julia Elizabeth*, which displays no feeling whatever for the stage.

But Paris was tending to stifle him and in a pathetic letter to Pádraic Colum at the end of the year he asked if Pádraic had written any poems:

> I got a dozen or so of poems in this foreign land and am astonished as if I'd had twins all by myself.

A fortnight later he wrote to Mr. Pinker and said that he was writing so little that he would not need a literary agent any longer.

From Paris he was keeping in touch with events at home. On 29 October 1913 he wrote to Bodkin strongly attacking Larkin's sentence. He was astounded that he should have been condemned to seven months' imprisonment. The attack on the clergy published in *The Irish Worker* in December[1] was written from Paris and Stephens still consulted A.E. on all important matters. On St. Stephen's Day he wrote to Bodkin to tell him that he had met Sir Frank Macmillan a few days before to discuss a new volume of verse for the spring. This came to nothing, probably because he had so little new work to offer; and the following February he wrote:

> I am afraid that as regards the verses which I sent to A.E. (*Songs from the Clay*) he was quite right in thumping me well. He did thump me, by the way, four pages of solid whacks was what he wrote me on these miserable poems. Since then I have transfigured them. I had a regular fury of verse & the book is

[1] See page 59.

no longer anything like what he saw. I do not think he would dislike it & now I think you also will be pleased at least with parts of it. The fault, as A.E. pointed out, was a lack of variety but thats not its fault now.

He was feeling more confident about his French at this time:

The french language is beginning to capitulate to me. Not in speech, for I never talk to anyone, but I read now with some ease & every week sees me better at that art. Anatole France is almost as easy reading as English.

He read a great deal of Anatole France and enjoyed him. In contrast he attempted Shakespeare but found him impossible.

On 28 April 1914, Stephens, feeling sentimental, asked Bodkin to send him a blackthorn stick, which he received soon: 'What a stick!' he wrote:

It's surely the champion of the world. It's the ideal and I have marched beside it to-day like a sapling strolling by an oak, I being the sapling. The Boulevard St. Michel admired me discreetly but passionately. Three jeunes gens came along swinging canes which were jewelled all down the front, but when they saw my stick they hid their canes and were abashed. I honestly can't tell you how pleased I am at your present, for I take it as a present, & it engraved & all in massy silver & with a ferrule on it would split a hill if it hit it. Myself & I have sworn Brotherhood, it snuggles into my hand as if that was its house planned by the gods . . . The douane man tried to pull its head off to see was there a sword inside it & he told me it was un tres dur canne begor.

He hoped to return to Dublin soon and, in June, he wrote to say that he had finished his new novel two days before, and therefore would not return to Ireland until 23 July. His return was then delayed by the illness of his children and other complications. Finally it was hastened by the impending war; and they arrived back on 2 August to stay in 2 Leinster Square, Rathmines.

'An Essay in Cubes', published in April of that year, gives no hint of the theosophical bias of his new novel. It is an essay in basic criticism, an analysis of what is essential to a good novel. Stephens had few theories about the art of prose writing other than his absolute ideals which applied to life as well as art. He thought that before laying down one's pen one should write the opening sentences of the next chapter in order to preserve the continuity, and another idea was 'rotation of crops', a method of distributing matter throughout a book, both of which practices may be deemed to have added to his novels. In this article, however, he condemned most novelists, classical and contemporary, by applying idealist principles to their work. The standard, he stated, was abominably low because, in general, writers of fiction neglected self-criticism. The majority had developed but one side of their nature, the intellectual or the emotional. The intellectual novelist distorted life, propounding a set of mathematical formulae where the aim was punishment of victims. The degree varied: Hardy depicted cruelty, protesting against its existence; but the opposite extreme could be illustrated by Meredith, who displayed no gift but merely the cruelty of his own mind in operation on his helpless creations. George Moore was one of the intellectual writers and should have been great, since he was free and self-conscious, but he lacked imagination which is essential for escape from environment. Imagination belonged to the emotional class of writer whom Stephens regarded as superior to the first since, though emotion is bound in ignorance, it is in itself wise. The trouble with emotion is that it is not conscious. Blake and Nietzsche, he believed, had developed both portions of their nature, balanced emotion and intellect, and were complete men, writing with their whole being.

He then turned to the critic, who, he said, should remember that he celebrated not a man, but a soul. The great critic found his food in the great novelist, was a great poet to boot, and so greater than all, but, he admitted, a man of this calibre had not yet lived. On summing up, judging every branch of writing, Stephens estimated that there had been no geniuses in fiction. Wordsworth, at his best, which was about five pages, was the highest product of English poetry, but he was no genius: genius, according to Stephens, chooses the crooked paths and this Wordsworth had not done. He borrowed the idea from a saying of Blake's which deliberately rejected the ideal state which Isaiah prophesied in Christ's Kingdom. In Christianity 'the crooked shall be made straight', but, in Blake, 'the crooked paths are the roads of genius', an image Stephens himself used in *The Crock of Gold* and 'The Goat Paths'. In this essay he applied the image to Blake himself:

> The tone of his mind was too metaphysical for poetic freedom; he did not entirely escape the petrifaction of intellect, although he nearly did; yet there are few poets who are better worth reading and few men whom one will love and respect more than he. If he was not a great poet, he was nearly a great man. There was life in that mind, and he was tortured as much in his being as in his verse; his verse is as crooked as his paths; his life was crooked; his whole being had a divine twist in it, and fame has curved away from him always.

Blake, Stephens said, was the only man who had trodden the crooked paths of genius.

John B. Yeats was taken with Stephens's article and wrote to W.B. supporting the former's view about self-consciousness; he declared that Stephens had vision, but that it was scarcely apparent, since he neglected the gift in order to pursue and chastise critics who ought to be left to settle their own disputes. 'Whether Stephens is a poet or a prose writer,' he wrote,

> turns upon whether or not he is enough self-centred to do his thinking and his feeling all by himself. If he cannot do his best without having some one to assail or cajole or persuade then he is of the prose writers—and only incidentally a poet. The true poet is all the time a visionary and whether with friends or not, as much alone as a man on his death bed . . .

The Demi-Gods shows Stephens in the double role of visionary and himself. It is a tale about two tinkers, Patsy and Mary, and their donkey, who find themselves suddenly joined in their wanderings by three archangels and, after the initial shock, gradually accept them as part of their responsibility. They walk through Donegal, Connemara and Kerry, and then return, ending their journey at the spot where they started. This, symbolically, completes the cycle of existence. Blake's attraction and repulsion are illustrated in the characters and further support the cycle symbol; in the group of three types, under-lining three absolutes, Finaun, the leader of the archangels, and the ass are soul mates and represent wisdom in particular; Caeltia, the second angel, and Patsy represent strength and ingenuity, while Mary and the youngest archangel, Art, are

66

Love. Mary finds kindred spirits in Finaun and the ass, but she
is irresistibly drawn towards Art. Patsy is at home with his own
equal Caeltia but is drawn towards Eileen, another character
in the book, who in turn falls for Art. The Three Absolutes here
are not stagnant as in *The Crock of Gold* but have come to
achieve a purpose, that of spreading peace; and one decides to
remain behind to fulfil himself in being, which he has never yet
experienced.

As a storyteller Stephens was more in his element than in *The
Crock of Gold*, and he indulged in frequent delays for philoso-
phizing. He had developed in other ways too. Continued intercourse with A.E. and contact with other like-minded men on
the occasions when he attended the Hermetic Society to hear
A.E. reading from the Indian Scriptures had roused his interest
in Theosophy and there are traces of it in his poetry though not
till *The Demi-Gods* can it be seen as something separate from his
Blakean philosophy. He already knew a great deal about
Madame Blavatsky from Russell, and about this time he had
been reading her more seriously—*The Secret Doctrine* is a difficult
book and in *The Insurrection in Dublin* he was still reading it—and
he then turned to Indian mystic writings.

Madame Blavatsky's cult of Theosophy had made a lasting
impression on the Anglo-Irish poets of the first generation, and
and its tenets helped to satisfy their spiritual cravings. These
were intensified by what seemed to them the smugness in
conventional religious persuasion. Theosophy is free enough in
doctrine, but it demands a personal devotion. For theosophists,
the goal in life is the unity of all living things in an Absolute
Being, and, to achieve this, life on earth must be spent in
attaining self-perfection through the inspiration of the divine
will. God is depersonalized and man must seek to depersonalize
himself and link the divine essence in his human personality
with its source, the one Reality.

The Dublin Lodge of the Theosophical Society had been
founded in April 1886 by Madame Blavatsky's *chela*, or disciple,
Charles Johnston. It was honoured almost at once by a visit
from Mohini Chatterjee, the famous Hindu theosophist; but it
did not come to public attention until about two years later,
when George Russell was becoming interested. It was then
that it became subject to misunderstanding and condemnation,

but it continued sporadically for about ten years. The programme of the Lodge consisted of three principles:

1. To form the nucleus of a universal brotherhood of humanity without distinction of race, creed, caste, sex or colour.

2. To encourage the studies of Eastern literature, philosophies, science and religions, and to indicate the importance of that study; and

3. To investigate the psychic powers latent in man, and the unexplained laws of nature.

Colonel Olcott, the President of the Theosophical Society and the most honest of its founder members, came to Dublin to lecture in 1889; and in 1892 the first edition of *The Irish Theosophist* appeared. However, the movement was too small, and was regarded too suspiciously by outsiders for it to flourish, and A.E.'s attempts to establish an Ideal 'Household', where a number of theosophically inclined men and women were to live together without friction and concern themselves with the task of self-perfection, came miserably to grief. After this A.E. realized that Theosophy must be the concern of the individual and indeed he, Yeats and Stephens developed their own conceptions of it in a personal manner. It was a private commitment and the society of like-minded people could only be artificial.

A.E. was the one who adhered most closely to the original principles of the Dublin Lodge. Though he regarded himself as a 'heretic' to Theosophy, he continued to hold its root doctrines and especially that of pantheism. Earth was the great mother of mankind, and he did not grow away from her as Wordsworth did, but felt closer to her as he became older. He read Indian, Persian, Judean and Greek philosophy and felt that all contained truth but that the Indian *Upanishads* and *Bhagavadgita* were the most interesting of all. He even decided to make use of his practical faculties in an inquiry into the relation of the politics of time to the politics of Eternity; for his philosophy based itself on the visions that he had of an ideal world. His chief emphasis was on the importance of Truth to the searching soul; and he felt that he not only benefited his soul, but strengthened his body by the practice of the presence of God. He was a practising Yogin, and, for a time, held two classes of instruction in Yoga each week.

He told me once that he had given up meditation on power as being too dangerous for a mere man until he had become more than something of a saint,

said Stephens in a broadcast about his friend.

Only the saint, he said, can handle power and be unharmed by it. I asked what had happened to make him quit? And he answered very simply that he found himself turning into power. That is, he was turning into fire. He was already a pillar of flame about twenty feet high, and he could hear himself as a rushing roar like the dreadful grumbling of half a Niagara. So he switched himself off in sheer terror lest he should in another second be just one calcined cinder which someone might carry away with a tongs. I blamed him there and then for not having dared the deed, and held that to be a cinder of that ilk was a far, far better thing than to be the editor of a barely wanted Irish weekly.

Yeats on the other hand was attracted to the Theosophical movement in an inquiring mood. 'Certainly if wisdom existed anywhere in the world,' he wrote about Madame Blavatsky, 'it must be in some lonely mind admitting no duty to us, communing with God only, conceding nothing from fear of favour.' He thought that the Theosophical doctrine of the Creation could have some truth in it:

> The wandering earth herself may be
> Only a sudden flaming word.

He, too, wished to found literature on the principles of Freedom, God and Immortality, but he required a more intellectual doctrine than A.E. did. Madame Blavatsky's confused account of the Creation soon ceased to interest him and he was evolving his own symbolism for the complexities of human consciousness in *A Vision*. The cycle of man's life before he attains perfection is minutely described and our variety of experience explained.

Stephens, as had been stated, was interested in *A Vision*, but he was not so intellectual as Yeats and his commonsense attitude to life led him to reject the mythologies of the older poets, and to pursue a philosophy which was possible for all men and not esoteric, and whose object was to train the character so that it might achieve final union with God.

Many of the beliefs he shared with Blake had common roots

with Theosophy; and there are the seeds of Theosophy in his early writings, for instance his declaration that Imagination stands rooted in truth. Imagination is to Theosophists the Divine Spirit. His commonsense was irradiated with his spiritual sense. 'Incognito', written in 1912, is the song of the Hidden God who can fill those aware of his presence with ecstasy, and in 'The Voice of God', and in other poems, his acknowledgement of the divinity in Nature also echoes Theosophical belief.

In *The Demi-Gods* he attempted an account of the Theosophical idea of evolution. It is contrasted with a hilarious account of chaos in the heaven and hell of rejected Christianity when the religion of reason finds itself faced with an unanswerable problem and all is confusion. There are seven orders of beings in Theosophy, the first four being human life in its various stages, while the last two have reached a stage of divinity. O'Brien is a being of the 'Fifth Round' and is growing towards complete spirituality. (Buddha was a 'Fifth Round' being). Owing to the evil he gathers through obstructing Art's work he becomes 'a fourth round life of the lowest globe'. This is how he comes on to the earth, as we are, for the most part, beings of the fourth round. Art, the youngest archangel, is an undeveloped divine creature, for he 'remembers more than one Day of a Great Breath, but he has no power for he has never had being, and so did not win to knowledge'. The very form of the journey in the book and the way the archangels leave as soon as they reach the point at which they started is reminiscent of Madame Blavatsky's cycles of existence. Stephens also described his view of the doctrine of Reincarnation: 'While generation succeeds generation a man has to fight the same fight. At the end he wins, and he never has to fight that battle again, and then he is ready for Paradise'; and this idea was behind his story of the Creation and the Fall. Long before the foundations of the world were laid, he said, two people came into being 'with the universe that was their shell'. They lived for myriads of existences in different forms always hating each other, yet desiring one another; fighting each other, fleeing each other, yet one needing the other all the time. Then stagnation came, 'they plumbed their desire and found wickedness glooming at the bottom, and they were conscious of themselves and of all

evil'. The demon was the accumulation of their evil and grew
as they lived, age after age. The man walked with the woman
under the apple trees until one day the woman became the
Devil's concubine and stole his energy. Then she found knowledge; and this caused her to send flowers to the man.

> The man, looking on these flowers, felt his heart move within
> him like water.
> 'Bring her to me,' said he to the demon.
> 'I will not do so,' replied the Misery.
> And, suddenly, the man leaped on the Spectre. He locked his
> arms about that cold neck, and clung furiously with his knees.
> 'Then I will go to her with you,' said he.
> And together they went headlong down the pit, and as they
> fell they battled frightfully in the dark pitch.

Stephens was still faithful to Blake, nevertheless, for the
woman does not achieve love and knowledge until she has
stolen energy from the demon.

Elsewhere Stephens was inaccurate in his detail of the first
creation according to Theosophists. His whole description of
the Creation, however, and the detailed events, is coloured with
a sense of levity and pure enjoyment which prove that it meant
little to him and that the mixed mythology of *The Demi-Gods*
was simply a convenient symbolism for what words could not
express. He illustrated the incomprehensibility of Divine Truth
when describing the archangels' conversation:

> The angels were wise, but in the vocabulary which they had
> to use wisdom had no terms. Their wisdom referred only to
> ultimates, and was the unhandiest of tools when dug into some
> immediate, curious problem. Before wisdom can be audible a
> new language must be invented, and they also had to unshape
> their definitions and retranslate these secular findings into terms
> wherein they could see the subject broadly, and they found that
> what they gained in breadth they lost in outline, and that the last
> generalization, however logically it was framed, was seldom
> more than an intensely interesting lie when it was dissected
> again. No truth in regard to space and time can retain virtue
> for longer than the beating of an artery.

Patsy and Mary are placed outside the chains of human
society, for, since they are really in touch with life and in the

freest condition which humans may experience, they can converse with beings who exist in true reality.

Unfortunately *The Demi-Gods* was not the tremendous success that *The Crock of Gold* had been, and in December Stephens wrote despondently to Bodkin about the reviews:

> They are not enthusiastic, but, with yourself, I believe in that book. The tepidity of those reviews sent me to re-read the book & it is, I'll swear, a good one, & almost worthy of having your name in its preface page. One gets terrified about dedications. Whenever I think of poor Stephen MacKenna I blush to think that I saddled my friend with that idiotic Lonely God. There are folk who laud that poem to my teeth.

The Stephenses had spent only a few months at home and returned to Paris, in spite of the War, arriving there on 3 November, after a weary journey—'Belgian refugees & French travelling with us in the boat & the word passport coming from every direction.' They found Paris sad. It was dull and empty now, and one could cross the street without taking one's life into one's hands. The atmosphere must have been depressing, for, in his letter, Stephens said he could write in Paris no more. He was no good at poetry, and he had made six abortive attempts at a new book.

His French, however, improved and he started to read Balzac, choosing *La Cousine Bette* first. He soon wanted more. By February 1915 he had read seven or eight of Balzac's books, including *Le Père Goriot*, *Ménage de Garçon* and *Illusions Perdues*, and depression had departed from him. His interest was caught by Balzac's style and technique, and 'his method of dealing with large masses of people and events'. He told Bodkin that he would now like to write 'le (sic) Comedie Humaine of Ireland':

> What a story there is to tell there. Ireland is & has been but 'is' for me who am modern and interested almost entirely in the things that I touch and feel. My plan is to take a slice of Irish time, say the twenty years culminating in this day & the to-morrow during which I will be writing and explore these, with the particularity of a grub working through an apple, until I have attained to a consciousness of Ireland in all its dimensions, and which consciousness I can impress, not alone into my books, but into our people—Behold a job!

The Insurrection in Dublin was a preliminary essay in this genre and his idea really developed when he attempted the 'comedie humaine' of Ireland in his reconstruction of the Táin saga. At this date, however, his plan was not too confident: 'I am a chasm of ignorance,' he wrote to Bodkin, 'and radiating from me are subterranean caves filled equally with ignorance.'

Songs from the Clay and *The Adventures of Seumas Beg* were both published this year and though still strongly influenced by Blake show him to be considering the elements in his own country which might be useful in his writing.

The titles of his books of verse indicate clearly Stephens's attitude in his work at the time of publication. The poems themselves in *Insurrections*, *The Hill of Vision* and *The Adventures of Seumas Beg* were all written in or around the same time and revised and arranged at the time of publication. They fall into two groups, those which have a traditional regular metre, one might almost say poetic exercises, and those which could be written by no one but Stephens himself. These are generally in an irregular, but rhyming, conversational metre, many starting in the middle of a monologue with 'and then . . .'. The line consists of eight or ten syllables, favourite lengths with the author, varied by shorter lines. 'Fossils' and 'The Shell' and 'Mac Dhoul', some of Stephens's best poems, belong to this group; while a few in regular metres reflect Stephens's unique powers of expression.

By the time *Songs from the Clay* was published, Stephens had completed his poet's apprenticeship, and felt he could at last pull the roots from the clay. The conversational method had clearly triumphed over the traditional, and the chanted poems bear witness to this fact. He was gentler, and perhaps more happy now than in the former books of poetry. 'The Satyr' is typical of his maturer style; for the poet is fascinated by the creature and describes him with apt wording, skilfully manoeuvred into a competent form, and this poem is an excellent example of his 'humour', in deep contrast to the work of the Metaphysicals, whose paradoxical wit he disliked. Insurrection had been abandoned for acceptance, but acceptance with understanding. He could search for the rabbit with the deepest of fellow feeling in its misery but he could not find it and so be of aid. Similarly he knew that the wind, the trees and the water had a message for him but he could not interpret it. On the other hand, though daylight is the background of sin, night always follows bringing rest and rebirth to all that was choked by day and this succession is inevitable. The earth is man's mother, God is his father, and therefore while mutual incomprehension continues among living things it is wise to preserve both love and hate, peace and strife, the parts which make up one's composition, in case by chance we discover when it is too late that we have rejected the wrong one. The stars and unearthly bodies must have to accept this state of affairs too since, though to all appearances they have attained heaven, something in earth attracts them without ceasing. Discipline, however, is important and we must abandon the clay whence we have come and walk forward bravely and unencumbered and by union with the sun 'catch at a spark from that primeval fire' which has also brought us into existence. For over all the moon shines, stating passively that there is no sin.

The moon influences the final passages of *The Adventures of Seumas Beg*, too, which, a simpler book, nevertheless had more impact. To make sure that it would not be received as a book for children Stephens enlarged it by adding *The Rocky Road to Dublin*. He realized how far removed he was from Dublin when writing to Bodkin about his new work:

> With *The Adventures of Seumas Beg* I am also issuing a collection of Dublin Sketches under the title of *The Rocky Road to Dublin*. My memory fails me a little far from my native land. I have remembered, for instance, that one walks in Grafton Street at four o'clock & have harvested that fact. I have remembered that flowerpots and patriotic verse fell from the windows of York Street, that one sees the moon well from Rathmines Bridge, that at Dumphies Corner you can get funereally tipsy & that King Billy rides in College Green & Larkin rides in Beresford Place. If you can recollect any small street facts & refresh my memories with your recollects I'll be your servant.

With *The Adventures of Seumas Beg*, this collection attempted a view of life completely innocent, unimpeded by prejudice or previous impression so that if life may not be seen as it really is, at least some room may be left for the opinion of others.

Stephens had lived on royalties throughout the period in Paris and it had been a hard struggle, with pinching when cheques arrived late. Depression set in when further articles were rejected: a series of nine or ten entitled 'Paris 1915', intended for and not accepted by the *Century Magazine*. Once more he felt that his inspiration was failing. On 16 June 1915, he wrote to Bodkin to say that he was looking desperately for a job. 'The months of this year still to come loom before this deponent with a bleak gaunt & hungry appearance,' he said. Nobody was interested in buying or reading his books. In the letter he enclosed an application form for the post of Registrar at the National Gallery in Dublin.

His letter of 9 July was a contrast, cheerful and optimistic, and Bodkin must have been confident that Stephens had secured the position. Stephens spoke of returning to Dublin. He said that Macmillans were bringing out *The Adventures of Seumas Beg* and he expected advance royalties. However, six days later, he wrote withdrawing his application for the clerkship in the National Gallery. His royalties had arrived and he enclosed a note for Bodkin to present to the Gallery, saying that owing to changed circumstances and a more comfortable income, he had decided to withdraw from the competition. In Bodkin's letter he explained that one of the Directors of the National Gallery was opposed to his appointment and, since Bodkin was sponsoring him, and was at the same time applying elsewhere for a post for himself, Stephens did not want prejudice against himself to turn into prejudice against Bodkin. A letter from Bodkin crossed with Stephens's letter in the post, in which was enclosed a cheque for fifteen pounds for Stephens's fare back to Dublin, a loan on the strength of his expected royalties. When replying to this on 16 July (Bodkin was always exceedingly generous and helpful to Stephens, and Stephens was scrupulous about repaying any loans) James Stephens named Dr. Mahaffy as the director who was opposed to him. Mahaffy was Provost of Trinity College at the time. A man of very decided opinion, he was also well known for his habit of living in the century that was past. On hearing the name James Stephens he assumed that the applicant for the job was the renowned Fenian James Stephens, and he abhorred and feared nationalism. He was aware, however, of Stephens's background and another reason for his opposition—Mahaffy was a snob— was that he did not wish a man from such humble origin to be appointed to such a post.

The efforts of Thomas Bodkin, Sarah Purser and the epicurean Bailey on Stephens's behalf, however, thwarted Mahaffy, and Stephens in gratitude accepted the post. His last letter to Bodkin from Paris, written in Paris and posted in London on 28 July (a Monday), said that he would arrive home on the following Thursday, and on 1 August 1915, he settled into his new position as Registrar to the National Gallery of Ireland.

V

Nationalism and the Irish Language

Gaelic is the most beautiful and expressive fashion of speech
in the whole world.

The Demi-Gods

BETWEEN the time when *Insurrections* was published and the
time he left Ireland for good were perhaps Stephens's most
exciting years, and he was happier than before. When they
returned to Dublin in 1915, he and his family settled into a
comfortable and more permanent flat in the city, on the top
floor of 42 Fitzwilliam Place, two doors down from the Purser
family; and, since Iris and Seumas were much the same age
as the Purser children, there was much coming and going
between the two houses. Seumas was a delightful small boy, a
miniature version of his father, though better-looking, with
curly dark-blond hair and hazel eyes. He and his sister went to
school at Nightingale Hall and later Seumas went to Earlsfort
House in Earlsfort Terrace. Seumas was a great favourite with
Dr. Bethel Solomons and would accompany him on his rounds,
visiting his patients, sitting up on the dickey of the cab, singing
happily.

The proximity of the Pursers' residence pleased Stephens.
He and his Irish terrier, who accompanied him everywhere,
would drop in in the evenings to chat with Mrs. Purser, who
was a member of A.E.'s Hermetic Society. He was reading the
Vedic Hymns, stimulated by A.E.'s studies, and he would
expound his spiritual notions to Mrs. Purser, sitting on a chair
with one leg under him and the other dangling, a bottle of stout
reposing at his elbow on the table beside him. He believed in
'young souls' and 'old souls', the latter being those who were
born with wisdom.

Confidence in his poetic gift revived again—he was full of

77

poetry and on occasion would wake Mrs. Stephens in the middle of the night to recite to her—and his conversational powers were once more in their element, with opponents to face him in a sparring match and *âmes sympathétiques* to aid him in building up the crescendo to a climax of verbal brilliance. At one Dublin party where about forty people were gathered, no one stirred or spoke, for the whole interest of the room was centred on the three figures of George Russell, Dr. Augustine Henry (the expert on Chinese flora and at this time Professor of Forestry in the Royal College of Science in Dublin) and James Stephens, standing in the middle of the room talking hard.

George Bernard Shaw invited himself to tea at 42 Fitzwilliam Place one day, but Stephens forgot to be there. When Shaw left at six o'clock they met on the doorstep. 'I don't like Parisian Irishmen,' said Shaw, who was affronted by Stephens's unpunctuality. 'And I hate Cockney Irishmen,' retorted Stephens. It is said that they continued to refer to each other as 'Mr.' for the rest of their lives, even though they were invited to the same parties and in effect made up the first disagreement.

There were other interesting figures too. G. K. Chesterton, of whom it is said that when he rose to offer his seat to a lady on the bus he might offer it to three, was introduced to him by A.E.; and in 1924, Bodkin brought him and Compton Mac-Kenzie together in what was to be a lifelong friendship. Seán O'Casey used to come to the Stephenses' 'evenings'. He was shy and never spoke, though he looked quite at home, and though he did not mention it then, he disliked what he felt was pretentiousness in the literary Dublin at the time. Stephens, however, was excepted. He used to get up on a high square stool in the sitting room to read his poetry, with simplicity, seeming completely unaware of any audience, and yet he wove a spell about the room with his words. Pádraic Ó Conaire was about Dublin in those days too. He had a desk up in the Gaelic League rooms where he would write his stories in between bouts of drinking. It was a common sight to see the queer little figure walking down Grafton Street unsteadily, looking for some one to lend him the money for more liquor, and calling out, 'Ah! there's Jimmy Stephens!' The other little figure, hearing the voice, in an instant would vanish swiftly round a corner.

Stephens still wrote to Thomas Bodkin frequently and on

every possible subject, on one occasion writing for the sheer joy of writing with a quill pen. They compared their reading, Bodkin lending Stephens books by writers such as Claudel, and they exchanged poems. They discussed A.E.'s ideas for an Irish anthology and they considered who should be asked to contribute. They also enjoyed reading French poetry and translating it, and Stephens later sent his translation of 'Heureux qui comme Ulysse', which they had worked on together in November, 1915, to *New Ireland*.[1] Bodkin was able to help Stephens with the legal side of publishing agreements. In 1916 he assisted in drawing up an agreement for the publication of *The Insurrection in Dublin*, and in the same year, on 4 August, Stephens wrote to Bodkin seeking a similar agreement for *Green Branches*. In June and July he sent Bodkin various versions of the poem, as he worked on them, two being sent on the same day; and he said that he had been to see 'Mr. Censor' about it, had had tea with him and that he had found him quite affable. He was able to return Bodkin's help in a different way by sending a testimonial for Bodkin's application for an Assistant Lectureship at National University.

A year or two afterwards, unfortunately, a rift came between Stephens and his friend, caused primarily by a clash of temperament, then widened through Bodkin's habit of cherishing resentments—he also had an uneven temper. Stephens remained friendly with Bodkin's relatives and acted as judge in a verse competition they held within the family, complimenting Thomas Bodkin's entry most highly. 'The least bad of these verses,' he summed up, 'is No. 4 & the next least bad is No. 3, and then, as T.B. says, in the order of descending villiany, comes 5, 2 and 1. No. 1 is of a real badness. It deserves a prize.' He and Bodkin were keeping in touch with one another, but from 1918 all Stephens's letters were official in their phrasing and there was a marked formality. He had been inclined to scribble drawings through his letters but after this they disappeared. On 19 October, 1918, he wrote to put off an arrangement to see Bodkin as the entire household, including the cats, and excluding himself, had Spanish 'flu. Communications henceforward were strictly businesslike, referring to Gallery meetings, the Lane pictures question, and so on.

[1] Published 25 August 1917.

Relationships of a deeper nature than that with Thomas Bodkin can ever have been were his attachments to Professor Osborn Bergin and, in especial, Stephen MacKenna, with whom he had common intellectual interests added to sensitivity and similar temperament. Bergin, a great authority in many subjects, inspired Stephens to learn to write music, but he admitted to finding the notes above the line very difficult. He attempted to play the concertina, which he called the 'squeegee', or sometimes 'the horror', but he later turned to the guitar with MacKenna and they took lessons from a teacher for a while.

Conversations about religion and literature were Stephens's and MacKenna's enjoyment and equally serious were conversations of a frivolous content. Stephens may have known the latter as early as 1909 or 1910; certainly he grew to know him well before the Paris period and, with his whimsy and good sense, he helped the mystic journalist, whose idealism had fired him to join the Greeks in their fight for independence, to keep his feet on earth. Stephens said to his friend once, partly in joke and partly in all seriousness: 'You read only your leading articles, so it is no wonder that you have no respect for current literature.'

Stephen MacKenna, strangely enough, though not so strange, it appears, if we had the opportunity of hearing him, was famed for his powers as a conversationalist in Dublin and was placed first among the great performers, excelling A.E. and Stephens in repute. Talk was a recognized skill in literary Dublin and the merit of each talker was discussed seriously. Imaginative power marked out one man above others. Stephens, in the days when he was broadcasting, was able to devote a whole broadcast to the art of conversation and describe the difference between the conversational styles of A.E., Yeats and MacKenna. 'Yeats was not the best of these,' he said, 'for his mind was always more at work than at play. He could surprise and inform you critically, but not creatively: for the creative act is always fantastic and flighty and almost unconcerned.' Fluency and the ability to talk at length on any subject was an important quality, and Stephens demonstrated it himself, as well as MacKenna's practice, which he commended, that of listening to others, and making them feel their own conversation to be as brilliant as his. Conversation was a natural gift and yet artificial in that Yeats and A.E. would plan subjects and their pronouncements on them for days before each 'evening'.

James Stephens was recognized as one of the giants of Dublin talk. Thomas McGreevy has described his talk as incantatory; in the middle of some apparent nonsense would come a flash of the vision of the universe. Norah Hoult once asked a new acquaintance of Stephens how they had conversed. 'He talked a lot about fleas,' she answered, 'of the marvellous precision with which they jumped.' Words were used extravagantly, poured on top of one another, and interchanged for full effect.

Recitation of poetry formed an important part of the 'evenings', and again the different styles were eagerly noted. Stephens regarded poetry not as a written but as an oral art, and his ideas on the reading of verse were general among Irish poets of his generation. It is difficult to know where he first adopted them, for in *Sinn Féin* in 1907, before he had met A.E. or Yeats, he was already insisting on song as the basis of poetry. All his life he held that music and verse were inextricably entangled. He said in his broadcasts during the 'forties that the actor should not read poetry for he is used to dealing in speech and will treat it as speech. 'Poetry is sound, not speech,' he stated, 'and the actor isn't skilled at all in sound.' For him the singer's art was much closer than the actor's to the spirit of poetry; and he urged readers to think of poetry as a thing without words and to listen to it in the same way that they listened to music:

> Verse has within it a much more subtle music than Beethoven or Mozart ever dreamt of, and unless the reader's voice gives verse that endless subtlety of music the poem doesn't come off . . . Here and there, there have been people, even in my lifetime who knew how to read. There was an old lady who lived away down in the West of Cork, and all the fiddlers of the neighbourhood used to go to hear her say certain poems, and then try and get it on to their fiddles, and they never could.

Yeats, A.E. and James Stephens were accustomed to repeat their new poems to people immediately after composing them, and Thomas MacDonagh examined the technique in his book, *Thomas Campion and the Art of English Poetry*, which he published in 1913. He made a distinction between song-verse, speech-verse and the third middle way in which the speech-element

81

and the song-element combine. He defined song-verse as consisting of rhythmic lines containing a number of units, the units
being in chronous periods. These recurring periods or time-
spaces are marked by word-accents, as in Hopkin's prosody.
He said that the harmonies may be complex, but on the few
occasions when Stephens sang his verse, the melody was simple.
Speech-verse is naturally much the same as song-verse except
that MacDonagh added another component, 'weight', a term
he adopted from Campion; and speech-verse was an important
method of versification among the Anglo-Irish poets, who took
it straight from Irish. In Irish verse, rhythms are less marked
because a line of poetry is measured by the number of its strong
syllables, and the number of weak syllables are not taken into
consideration. The effect is of a slower, more wandering sound,
which is close to the rhythm of prose. The third type of verse
named by MacDonagh is akin to 'chant'. MacDonagh believed
that it owed its origin 'either to the invention of tone-deaf
poets, or of poets who, though highly musical, compose their
verse through chanting rather than through song'. He cited
Yeats as one of the tone-deaf, or rather 'tune-deaf', poets, and
indeed Yeats and A.E. believed that Homer chanted in this
method, and that it was a tradition dating back to before the
days of the modern musical scale. MacDonagh experimented on
both A.E. and Yeats to test the soundness of his theory. He
listened to Russell reading some poems of Shelley, Yeats,
Milton, Walt Whitman, Keats and Swinburne, together with
'As Ye Came from the Holy Land of Walshingham':

> He recited these from memory, untroubled by the printed text,
> and in all of them he gave to each word, and to each line, its
> due value and verse music. Mr. Russell is tone-deaf. He chants
> verse on a few notes, rising and falling with the emotion. Mr.
> James Stephens, who came in also, and I, both of musical ear,
> found that, when we did not merely say verse, we chanted it on
> a monotone, or, if we chanted otherwise, the changes that we
> made seemed to be directed by musical ideas or memories.

Stephens was clearly affected by these experiments and he
developed his own version of chanting. I have not heard A.E.
reading his verse, but Yeats's method certainly did not resemble
that of James Stephens at all. He gave more tone to the vowels
than English poets do, but his chanting sounded reedy because

the notes he used had no musical significance. Stephens, on the other hand, while also employing few notes, invested in them the same musical quality as a priest chanting Mass. They were definite notes of the scale and were richly rounded. His rhythms, too, were those of barred music, and did not wander as those of the other poets did. Yeats read his verse, without exception, in his chanting. But Stephens read in two contrasting styles, depending on content, one being treated as speech-verse and the other as chant. In 'The Goat Paths' he used both methods; he recited at first in a conversational way, but uttered the last stanza like an incantation:

> I would think
> Until I found
> Something
> I can never find;
> —Something
> Lying
> On the ground
> In the bottom
> Of my mind.

Dublin was tense with nationalist feeling at this time, though nobody dreamed that for a week she would be the scene of active warfare, and James Stephens must have derived much inspiration from his association with MacKenna whose experience of the struggle for freedom abroad had had no taint of sentimentality. It may have been about this time that he went to the Kerry Gaeltacht to practise speaking Irish, which he was now studying in earnest, for in a letter to Edward MacLysaght, on 25 September 1916, he stated that his love for Ireland was separate from politics and was being deepened through scholarship:

It was very kind of you to send me your book. I delayed writing as I wished to read you first. I am now in the centre of the book. I know from it a good deal about Couperin that I did not know before & a good deal about yourself. It is a very fine thing for our country that books like this should be written and I hope you will write many of them. We ought all to be thinking about every plane & surface & depth of Ireland, so as to have some real knowledge of her rather than the sentimental or the patriotic guessing which has served us up to the present.

The Insurrection in Dublin published that year, summed up the state of affairs in Ireland with some tentative notes for a new policy. Through A.E. he had learnt much about co-operative schemes for Ireland, and through Thomas MacDonagh, Pearse and Colum about the political schemes; yet *The Insurrection in Dublin* is quite objective in its approach, and he had reached the point where he deliberately dissociated himself from his former enthusiastic support of James Connolly's labour movement and, though still in complete sympathy with the dilemma of the working classes and with the insurgents, he could evaluate Connolly's aims, and commend his intellect and the benefit of his practical thinking to the Volunteer force in Dublin, while stating that politics were not his concern. Sentiment was muted in a viewpoint which was wider than that of 'Irish Englishmen', for he now combined an understanding of the attitudes of both North and South with a belief that no solution could be reached until each side had progressed a little. He had felt very emotionally in the days of *Sinn Féin*. Feeling was strong in his article in *The Irish Worker*, in 1913, where he savagely attacked the Catholic clergy in Dublin for their attitude to the Strike, and Pearse, who was not inclined to draw sectarian distinctions in political and social disputes, and who was sympathetic towards Larkin and the strikers, thought that 'for a Protestant Stephens had gone much too far'. Stephens also told Laurence Easterbrook whom he met at Bay Colthurst's house that he had been making himself ill with hatred for England at one time and that it had gone so far as to interfere with his work in the Gallery. But his fresh view, while still fervently patriotic, was linked with his sense of humour when he exclaimed: 'Ha! we'll show the rotten English what education is when we can run our own country.' In his preface to MacDonagh's *Poetical Works* too, written in the August after MacDonagh died, he made it clear that the work of the Volunteers was not his business and did not enter into their private conversation, and that on the last occasion that they had met MacDonagh chided him playfully with: 'When are you lads going to stop writing stories and do something?'

The Insurrection in Dublin was written objectively, in an effort to assess the initial cause of the Rising and its resultant effect on the political situation, so that some unbiassed solution might

James Stephens by Estella Solomons, A.R.H.A.

Thomas Court.

42 Fitzwilliam Place (third door from left).

suggest itself to the powers involved. He resorted to the mock heroic, which he often adopted when equipped with a particularly workable theme for a story, pausing to observe with delight the technique of another storyteller who spread wild rumours of every nature about the horrors:

> He made these things up in his head. Then he repeated them to himself in a loud voice, and became somehow persuaded that they had been told to him by a well-informed stranger, and then he believed them and told them to everybody he met . . . A singular man truly, and as I do think the only thoroughly happy man in our city.

The narrative is most leisurely and detailed, with frequent references to his own work and preoccupations and to those of other citizens, which make evident the remote nature of the movement. This is a first-hand account of the Insurrection of 1916, but it is also the journal of a professional writer, well aware that his private life and opinions will be of interest to the public. He was never to reveal himself so plainly again in his work; but, utterly serious in the conclusion, he suggested that an authoritative account remained to be written, in place of this tentative study by an individual. He himself laid the blame for the Insurrection on John Redmond for pledging Ireland's support to England in the Great War without the agreement of his countrymen, when neutrality was all that he had a right to offer; the ultimate blame, he said, belonged to England, who had always exploited Ireland and never encouraged her potentialities in any way, and he urged all Irishmen to join together in ending this unhappy state by building a concrete future for Ireland founded on the idealism of those who had sacrificed themselves.

Green Branches, published a few months later, and not one of his great poems, also reflects this professional manner and is an attempt at a classical lament. The verse is beautifully modulated in traditional vein, mourning the departed dead, and he emphasizes that their death is a prelude to life and therefore their memory will flourish for evermore. Their death, too, is the opening to a great future for Ireland:

> Joy be with us, and honour close the tale;

Now do we dip the prow, and shake the sail,
And take the wind, and bid adieu to rest.

With glad endeavour we begin the quest
That destiny commands, though where we go,
Or guided by what star, no man doth know.

Uncharted is our course, our hearts untried,
And we may weary e'er we take the tide,
Or make fair haven from the moaning sea.

Be ye propitious, winds of destiny,
On us at first blow not too boisterous bold;
All Ireland hath is packed into this hold,
Her hopes flies at the peak. Now it is dawn,
And we away. Be with us Mananaun.

Stephens once showed Seán MacGiollarnath a scrapbook into which he had pasted all the newspaper pictures he had collected of the battles and of the destruction of Dublin buildings, and these must have helped him in his account of the Insurrection. His position of detached recorder was apparent again in a brief note to MacGiollarnath in 1917 where he reiterated his tribute to James Connolly in *The Insurrection in Dublin*. Jim Larkin's propagation of pure socialist ideals and his winning personality and handsome appearance had perhaps had more instant impact on Dublin than had Connolly's work but Stephens had a deeper admiration for Connolly's brilliant mind and for his decision to relate the fights for political independence and for social advance:

> Thanks for the pamphlet on Connolly. I read it through at a sitting. I think you are right in saying that with the passing of Connolly there has passed one of the greatest assets Ireland had, and I think you are right in prophesying that neither he nor his teachings will be forgotten. It may seem that all will have to be recommenced, but even tho' it does not yet appear, he dug deeper than he knew and has laid strong foundations.
>
> The pamphlet as well as being written with great interest, is written with great fairness, and does give to the uninitiated the trend of that great combat which began in 1913 and wont end at Tibb's Eve. We want Larkins and Connollys here in Ireland and we want Sean MacGiollarnaths also, but we are not bankrupt yet, tho' the list was so summarily curtailed.

His desire to build a new Ireland was subordinated to his writer's ambition, indeed was a product of the will to be a great writer, and this is very evident in the placing of emphasis in his words to MacLysaght: 'There are . . . more than a thousand things I would like to talk to you about on the subject of writing. As regards co-operation you have me skinned . . .'

It is interesting to pause for a moment and compare the difference in attitude of Stephens and W. B. Yeats. Yeats, always governed by poetic intellect, maintained his aloofness from the days when he supported the movement for independence to the days when he became a Senator of the Free State, and he exalted to an abstraction the 'terrible beauty' of the Insurrection. Stephens, on the other hand, had involved himself emotionally at first, and had come to realize that emotion is not sufficient in dealing with political issues. He withdrew, content to erupt occasionally with patriotic sentiment, to offer opinions based on sound commonsense, but determined to devote his pen to the subjects he now knew were really near to his heart.

During the Troubles he joined a class for beginners of Irish in the branch of the Gaelic League in Ely Place. A detective stood outside the door for the students' protection but in those turbulent days the interest of the work was all that the students remembered. Patrick O'Sullivan, who afterwards went out to teach English in Germany, gave the classes and George Moore's brother, Colonel Maurice Moore, with his sister and niece were also in the class. The adult students prepared grammatical exercises and learned poetry by heart phonetically. They learned 'Humpty Dumpty' in Irish.

> Bhí Humpty Dumpty 'na shuidhe ar an bhfalla.
> Do shéidh an ghaoth is thuit ar an dtalamh;
> Do cnapadh a phlaosc is briseadh a chroí
> 'Dtí go raibh se bán.   Anois tá sé buidhe.
>
> Tháinig amach an seana-bhean liath
> Is connaic sí Humpty Dumpty ina luí.
> 'Anois' ar sise 'ní féidir leis an rí
> Ní an méid capall is feara 'tá faoi
> Humpty Dumpty a chur arís mar a bhí.'

Stephens from the first took well to the Irish language and

in it found a fresh source of inspiration and themes for his stories, which was strengthened by his taste for and affinity with the Old Irish narrative method. He arranged additional tuition with his friend Seán MacGiollarnath. MacKenna and Osborn Bergin helped him greatly, and, in 1917, he wrote to MacLysaght in great excitement saying that through Professor Curtis, he had discovered Joseph Dunn's edition of the Táin.[1] This gave him the basis for two new books, and the skeleton for more if he had had the impetus to continue. His reading of Irish poetry yielded his best book of verse, *Reincarnations*, published in 1918. *The Crock of Gold* and *The Charwoman's Daughter* had been full of native expression and traditions of Irish culture and legend were assimilated into the narrative; *The Irish Review* and *Sinn Féin* had given Stephens direct contact with Irish customs and poetry. Articles of topical interest appeared in both, for example, a history of the Irish people, and there were stories and essays in Irish itself. He had read translations and adaptations of Irish verse by MacDonagh and other friends, and later in the Cuala Press broadsheets, and he had rewritten two of Kuno Meyer's translations in straight-forward English metre, which bore no resemblance to and failed to recapture the atmosphere of the originals, publishing them as 'King and Hermit' and 'Oisín and Niamh' in *Sinn Féin*. But now he was at grips with genuine Irish and had the opportunity of discussing intricate points with Dr., or 'Blessed' Bergin, as he affectionately called him, and Edmund Curtis and Stephen MacKenna, all celebrated scholars. MacKenna indeed held Irish evenings at his house when nothing but Irish was to be spoken. If an Irish word was not known, the French or German equivalent might be substituted, but English was altogether taboo. Stephens had already acquainted himself with Hyde's work and the more popular publications of Lady Gregory, T. W. Rolleston and others, and editions of Irish stories appeared frequently with translations facing each page of text. He used the Irish Texts Society editions of Ó Bruadair's poems and *Dánta Aodhagáin Uí Rathaille* ('The Poems of Egan O'Rahilly') and Douglas Hyde's *Abhráin atá leagtha ar an Reachtuire* ('Poems ascribed to Raftery') as his material for *Reincarnations*.

[1] Letter, 20 April 1917 (National Library of Ireland).

It was from the last that he derived most for his book. Ó Bruadair and O'Rahilly were learned men whose intellectual training contributed a great deal to the ideas they expressed. Ó Bruadair, too, was born at the end of the bardic period and so his work contains much of the academic wit, the complicated verse structure and refined imagery of the bardic school. Raftery, however, was an uneducated countryman with a natural gift for poetry, and on some occasions his verse cannot be excelled for its simplicity of beauty. As well as this, it was passed down by word of mouth, and many versions of his poems are extant, so that the adapter has a freer hand than with the classical poems of Ó Bruadair and O'Rahilly. Stephens himself said that readers could not criticize Raftery but could only say how much they loved him. He himself had the closest acquaintance with Raftery's work and treated it as he wished, unconstrained by any feelings of deference.

His method varied from development of an idea to direct translation. One of his early enthusiasms, which had soon died, had been for Greek verse (in translation), and he had treated the scraps of Sappho similarly, blowing up a phrase or a sentence into many verses with indifferent success; but now he really broke through to the heart of the inspiration of each poet and knew each character intimately as his friends. O'Rahilly's wistfulness and longing for a time that was gone would have struck a note of romance for him, and Raftery had the freedom and beauty of nature at his fingertips; while it is unnecessary to point out why he chose the irrepressible Ó Bruadair. 'Ó Bruadair lets out of him an unending rebellious bawl which could be the most desolating utterance ever made by man if it was not also the most gleeful,' he wrote. Stephens understood every trick of mood or depression that the poets reflected and made them his own, and in this stood apart from the accurate, objective translators. MacDonagh attempted the original Irish rhythm, assonance and rhyme in some of his translations but the result was unconvincing, and he failed to recapture the richness and song of the Irish. No one was successful in handling this form of versification until Austin Clarke. It is only in the dignified simplicity of Colum's 'She Moved Through the Fair', an original composition, or some passages in Synge's *Deirdre* that we see any resemblance to Stephens's restrained yet poetic mode of speech, in which he made the literature of the past live again for an age of different ideals.

In his adaptations Stephens was at his best when he picked what pleased him out of a poem and ignored the rest. He brought two outstanding qualities to his translations, imagination and brevity. He realized that what suited one age would have no special appeal for modern society, so in metre and length he adapted the older poems to the idiom of the twentieth century. He contracted long drawn-out emotion and drew attention to one idea where two or three were offered formerly, for he was consciously a poet and not a preserver of tradition for sentimental reasons. From the seven verses in Hyde's translation of the beautiful Máire Ní hEidhin he chose only one and the transformation is startling. Hyde wrote:

> It is beautiful and airy on the side of the mountain
> Looking down on Ballylee
> Walking in the glen picking nuts and berries
> And hearing the bird's music and fairy songs.
> What meaning has all this until you get a sight
> Of the blossom of the branches beside it;
> It is no good denying it and don't hide it from anyone,
> She is the sky of the sun and the love of my heart.

Stephens's version is a completely new poem:

> She is the sky of the sun,
> She is the dart
> Of love,
> She is the love of my heart,
> She is a rune,
> She is above
> The women of the race of Eve
> As the sun is above the moon.
>
> Lovely and airy the view from the hill
> That looks down Ballylee;
> But no good sight is good until
> By great good luck you see
> The Blossom of the Branches walking towards you
> Airily.

VI

Irish Epic

More than eight hundred years ago a famous saint informed
the world that the language spoken in heaven was Gaelic, and,
presumably, he had information on the point. He was not an
Irishman, and he had no reason to exalt Fodhla above the
other nations of the earth, and therefore, his statement may be
accepted on its merits, the more particularly as no other saint
has denied it, and every Irish person is prepared to credit it.

The Demi-Gods

THE job in the National Gallery, though it did not tie Stephens
greatly, overworked him since the Director was away frequently
and the burden of the responsibility fell on the registrar. He had
left his Paris flat in 1915 when the fighting was not too bad but
returned for holidays at intervals. Mrs. Stephens would go
ahead a few days in advance to open the flat and put it in order,
and Stephens would follow, making a practice of dining with
Thomas McGreevy in the Marine Hotel before he boarded the
boat. Life was very full with his job, Paris and writing; Stephens
had never been strong, and his health grew more delicate. In
January 1917 he had influenza very badly, and later the same
year he had the first of a series of operations which were to take
place in the coming years. However, on this occasion his friends
came to his aid and Bethel Solomons raised a small fund for
him:

"I was speaking to A.E. the other day about James Stephens",
he wrote to Edward MacLysaght on 15 March 1917, assuring
him that Stephens knew nothing about his plans,

and having consulted his doctor, who considers that James
should go away in order to recruit his health, we found that it
would be necess. to collect £21 so that he might have this
holiday. We decided therefore to ask seven or eight of his

intimate friends to give £3 each. You are one of those we thought we might bother. Stephens as you know has had heavy expenses. His royalties are down and his salary is small.

Stephens went to Enniskerry with his wife to stay at Cookstown Hotel for a fortnight. But it cannot have been as restorative as his friends wished for it snowed all the time, and Cynthia had an abscess and neuralgia. She too was not strong and many of Stephens's letters refer to her being indisposed.

He still lived quietly when in Paris, as his French was never perfect, though he had become more fluent, and despite his early interest in Balzac he had no great taste for French literature. He drank little and did not frequent the literary cafés, but was, in a way, a recluse. 'One can starve very well on French bread,' he would say. The American writer, Paul Scott Mowrer, used to meet him for lunch at a modest Italian restaurant hidden away in the Passage Choiseul, where Stephens would talk or recite in an ever-flowing monologue, probably overjoyed to be with someone who could understand him.

> He was not much concerned with the war. He was more given to expatiating on Cuchulain and Angus than on Joffre or Foch. His mind ran mainly to literature and the mysteries of the human soul. To hear him, Ireland was the most ancient and only authentic seat of culture, from which all others had brazenly borrowed; and never in Athens or Rome, Paris or London, had there been aught to equal the intellectual and artistic life that flourished in Dublin. No Englishman knew how to write, and, of course, no Frenchman.[1]

His affection for his friends in Dublin never died when he was away; and when a Parisian bus passed, Stephens would point at the registration on it, 'Look, that's Russell's bus—A.E.'

The small income from his books sometimes gave out towards the end of the month. When he came to his last gold louis, instead of stretching it out to make ends meet, he would take his wife to the Italian restaurant for a supper of lobster and Asti Spumanti, then drop in on Scott Mowrer the next day to borrow a few francs to tide him over. He always paid off his debts with meticulous care.

[1] *The House of Europe* (Houghton Mifflin), 1945, p. 267.

During 1918, Stephens was writing once again. The despair of 1914 was gone; he had recovered his fluency since his return to Dublin and had already written some of the short stories which were to appear in *Etched in Moonlight*. Now the whole of his attention was directed upon the *Táin Bó Cuailnge*. He intended to devote five volumes to the famous epic, and continued to tell his friends of this plan, though in fact he completed only two; but he first envisaged it as a play, the 'comedie humaine' he had described to Bodkin, worked in terms of mediaeval Ireland, and he wrote a draft of the plot, now to be found in the New York Public Library. Twenty years later he thought of it as a subject for the screen. This too came to nothing. But his detailed study of Dunn's translation of the epic gave him complete command of the material for *Deirdre* and *In the Land of Youth*.

The *Táin Bó Cuailnge* tells how Maeve, Queen of Connaught, led the men of Connaught in war against the men of Ulster in an attempt to obtain the Brown Bull of Cuailnge. The first page of Stephens's *Scenario*[1] bears the frivolous sentence; 'The milk supply was organized in weekly supplies by Flidais Foltcain (Lovely Hair) wife of Ailill Finn'; and in the following pages he noted with care any humorous incidents which took his fancy, such as Darè's bound of joy on hearing the terms Maeve offered in exchange for the Brown Bull, which caused his bed to break in two. The notes however are painstaking and thorough and are indebted to other sources besides Dunn. Dunn's index of place and personal names at the end of the book was invaluable for the explanations included, and in a lengthy introduction he outlined the plot of the saga with some background material which again could not be neglected. Stephens gathered together all the information he found about each character, Conall Cernach, Cuchulain, Laeg, Conor, Maeve, Ailill[2] and others, with details of their appearances, their family and marriage connections and their mode of dress. Colours in particular delighted him, and odd descriptions. He then outlined the story of the Táin, or Cattle Raid, in sixteen chapters, starting with one page to each chapter. He divided

---

[1] Dated 25 July 1918.
[2] 'Ailill', for some reason, he wrote as 'Oilioll' almost consistently through the *Scenario*. He is correctly 'Ailill' in *In The Land of Youth*.

this in two, giving the events briefly at the top of the page, and below the centre line providing dialogue and further elaboration, lapsing into shorthand when a particularly pungent phrase came to him. Gradually the detailed section swelled as he progressed so that Chapter Seven, which describes the manner in which Cuchulain killed his opponents, consisted of nine pages of tiny writing. The whole draft is a lively and interesting account, though in many places illegible.

Meanwhile he published his short story 'Hunger',[1] receiving £10 for six month's copyright from the Sign of the Three Candles Press, and it sold out almost immediately. The story is similar to that in *The Crock of Gold* and is a further example of Stephens's imagination recreating reality; for he himself had experienced this suffering at close quarters, and he had a deep concern for the needy and abhorred their poor conditions of work. The epigraph is a quotation from the Old Irish *Triads of Ireland*:

> Tri caindle forosnat cach ndorcha: Fír, aicned, ecna.
> Three candles which lighten every darkness: truth, nature,
>   wisdom.

Colm O Lochlainn, director of the Sign of the Three Candles, was struck by the diminutive author, whom he had met first at Dr. Curran's house. Stephens visited him with Darrell Figgis one evening, and O Lochlainn opened the door to see Stephens dancing in the moonlight round a holly tree on the lawn.

One of his interests was the Dublin Drama League, founded towards the end of 1918 by Yeats, to take the place of the former Hardwicke Street Theatre. The Abbey Theatre was concentrating on Irish plays and cottage drama, and so intellectual circles felt a great need to see contemporary European and classical plays. Yeats was President, Stephens was Vice-President, and Lennox Robinson became Secretary. They performed in the Abbey Theatre on Sunday night, plays were only permitted to run for two performances, and guest actors came from the Abbey to play the leads while the Arts Club provided the chorus and filled 'walk-on' roles. There were also play-readings and reading of verse for members of the League. The first play was performed in February 1919, and

[1] Published in 1918.

during the ten years that the League survived, the Gate
Theatre afterwards taking its place, plays by Strindberg,
Tchekov, Eugene O'Neill, Euripedes, Dunsany, Shaw, Cannon,
Jules Romain, Flecker, Sierra and Chesterton, among others,
were performed. Lennox Robinson often produced them. *The
Wooing of Julia Elizabeth* was given its last performance by the
Drama League, in August 1920. Stephens's interest, however,
confined itself to encouragement of dramatics for he wrote no
more for the stage, devoting himself to working his interpreta-
tions of Irish saga.

He was feeling his responsibilities now and on the 14 May
1919, he married Cynthia in the Register Office in the District
of St. Giles in London. (Her husband must have died about
this time and left Mrs. Kavanagh free at last.) She is described
as a widow aged thirty-two on the marriage certificate. Stephens
gave his age as thirty-six, though he was really thirty-nine.
Then at the end of the following year he made his will leaving
all he had to Seumas and Iris and Mrs. Stephens; his wife and
Thomas Bodkin were to be literary executors, but any selection
of his poetry for publication was to be left to the discretion of
Bodkin and A.E.

Poetry was the only medium in which he felt his imagination
had full play and after this he published only three important
prose works. During the nineteen-twenties he used to visit the
Colthurst family at Lucan House near Dublin. Captain R. St.
J. J. Colthurst, 'Bay' Colthurst, was the second son of Sir
George Colthurst of Blarney. Stephens was adored by the
children of the family, who saw the likeness of two leprechaun
horns in the two little dents in his forehead, and there was a
little wizened thorn tree in Phoenix Park which they called
James Stephens to his great amusement. He would go for walks
with them, accompanied by the enormous Irish terrier which
had adopted him and his family, and play all kinds of imaginative games or write poems for them on slips of paper. The
reading aloud of his manuscripts as he had written them was
inevitable and everyone listened eagerly as he sat by the fire in
the library, sometimes carried away in his reading, and acting
the parts of his characters. A.E. used to come too and there
would be heated discussions until the early hours of the morning
about their souls, or the esoteric significance of the seven-

pointed star, and so on. One morning at about two o'clock, after one of these sessions, Stephens remarked, 'Well, I know what is holding me back. It's women.' 'Surely you can cure yourself of that,' said someone. 'I know,' said James, 'But you see I don't want to'—a typical Stephens remark, true to a point, yet extravagant in its irrelevance.

They were drafts of the stories for his Irish tales that the Colthurst family heard Stephens reading. *Irish Fairy Tales* was published in 1920. Pádraic Colum has quarrelled with the title as he thinks it is inaccurate, for the originals belonged to the repertoire of the professional story-tellers and reflected aristocratic and not folk life. The stories in this book are not fairy-tales in the strict sense of the word, but it is worth noting that they are not heroic tales either. The majority of them come from the Fenian cycle, romantic mediaeval tales whose theme develops from a joy in the physical beauties of life, and does not extol a heroic code of conduct. But Stephens intentionally wove a fairy-tale atmosphere about his retelling of these stories by omitting the parts that dealt with the physical side of sex. He was not afraid of sex, and in his description of the lusts of Conachúr, in *Deirdre*, threw more light on the king's character. His description in *In The Land of Youth* of Étain's physical passion for Ailill, and disgust at herself, while yet assuring us of the innocence of her intentions is most skilfully managed. Life in *Irish Fairy Tales*, however, is elevated to the symbolic plane of that in the Many-Coloured Land, the mythological world which is one step beyond the Shí, where all conception is chaste. In 'The Wooing of Becfola' Dermod marries the unknown woman who has come across the sea and 'it was part of their understanding that they should live happily ever after'.

Many passages of *Irish Fairy Tales*, with no original at all, sound as if they had been translated directly from a twelfth-century text. In other cases the original (he used the text in *The Voyage of Bran and the Celtic Doctrine of Rebirth* by Kuno Meyer and Alfred Nutt[1]) sounds as if it had been created by Stephens himself—

> there was not a bone of his of the size of an inch, but was filled with love of the girl.

[1] *The Voyage of Bran and The Celtic Doctrine of Rebirth*, by Kuno Meyer and Alfred Nutt (2 vols.), London, 1895 and 1897.

He could introduce a direct translation of an Irish idiom or one of the native terms of affection, such as 'The Cluster of Nuts', or 'The true Blossom of the Branches', into his prose without fear of archaism or awkwardness, as the spirit of his style is extremely close to that of the original. All the things that delight Finn as related in the Fenian poems, the cry of the hounds and so on, delighted Stephens himself personally. He could expand the original or contract it with equal success. The description of 'The Carl of the Drab Coat', which is absurdly long and extravagant in the original, is cut by half. In this and the other late Fenian tales Stephens kept most closely to the text. The tendency in fifteenth- and sixteenth-century Irish prose was to load the writing with more and more images and adjectives so that it is almost impossible to read, and Stephens, far from having to embroider on his original, used his discretion in omitting the long lists of men present at feasts, the superabundance of adjectives, and the horrid descriptions of manglings. He made the understatement, typical of the mediaeval Irish style, part of his own expression, and used to the full two other features of Fenian prose, alliteration and internal rhyme in consecutive words. While developing the ancient tales for his own use, he was anxious to be as accurate as he could. Sometimes he mentioned that the version of a tale he narrated might be incorrect. He attempted a rough approximation of the modern Irish pronunciation of names of places and people. However, here the limitations of his scholarship are plain, for he had no satisfactory standard by which to judge the names, and in names which are uncommon or non-existent in Modern Irish and thus have no modern equivalent, he was sometimes altogether wrong. It would be interesting to know where he found justification for 'Fionn the son of Uail', which in every instance is Fionn mac *Cumhail*. Perhaps he ran the 'C's' together as in MacCushin (Mac Oisín) in *The Crock of Gold*. His attempts at philological analysis were curiously naïve: how can 'London' be supposed to derive from 'Dun Lúigh'?

In each of his three new books he displayed, almost as if they were the result of experiments, a different approach to the material. In *Irish Fairy Tales* the matter is idealized, creating a make-believe atmosphere. *In the Land of Youth* attempts to sort out some of the complicated *Rémscéla*, or fore-tales to the *Táin*

Bó Cuailnge, explaining the origin of the bulls among other things and illustrating the various characters involved. But *Deirdre*, which was designed in the first place to show why Fergus, an Ulsterman, was the unwilling companion of Maeve in the Connacht raid on Ulster, is detached from the main epic and treated for its own literary value, in the tradition of the Anglo-Irish school, who have always ignored its place in the *Táin Bó Cuailnge*. Stephens was interested in the psychological cause of the tragedy and cast it in a modern vein instead of romanticizing it as his contemporaries did.

His treatment of his sources in *Irish Fairy Tales* was similar to that in the other two books, though there are one or two inaccuracies which look like mere carelessness. In general he followed the original text as far as detail was concerned and developed incidents, adding ideas of his own where suitable. He straightened out the complexities which are inevitable where a fragmentary tale is all that survives, or where details hold up the narrative and are irrelevant. In the narration of the reincarnations of Tuan, he followed his own instinct in simplifying the events, thus achieving a better woven tale. In *Tochmarc Becfhola*, taken from the edition by Standish O'Grady in *Silva Gaedelica*, there is an interval of a year between Becfhola's attempted elopement and the arrival of the clerics but Stephens retold events as happening on the same day and so made it more dramatic. 'Mongan's Frenzy' is a remoulding of two separate texts, *Baile Mongáin* and *Compert Mongáin*, to make one story. *Baile Mongáin* tells how Findtigernd, Mongan's wife, beseeches her husband to relate his adventures. He asks for a respite of seven years. When the time arrives they are at the hill of Usnech in Meath. A great hail-storm comes on them and Mongan, his wife and some companions find themselves in Faery, before a beautiful house. Inside the house is a sumptuous feast.

> Seven vats of wine there were. Mongan was made welcome in the house. He stayed there. He became intoxicated. It was then and there that Mongan sang the 'Frenzy' to his wife, since he had promised he would tell her something of his adventures.

Then they awake in Rathmore and find that they have spent a year in Faery. *Compert Mongáin ocus serc Duibe-Lacha do Mongán,* a separate story, is the tale of Mongan's adventures, and Stephens inserts it in its place, Mongan relating the story during the course of the banquet.

Stephens had very distinct views on the art of story-telling, and was interested in every aspect, even, as we have seen, examining the way in which rumours spring up out of nothing, in *The Insurrection in Dublin*. He felt that a tale belonged to any one who cared to make anything of it. *In the Land of Youth* has a scientific approach to the story-teller; in relating the tale Stephens showed how the mediaeval audiences regarded a *seanachaidhe* objectively and praised the tale, not the inventor of it. In addition, Fergus, Ailill and Maeve discuss methods of story-telling abstractly, and at the same time demonstrate, by their disagreement over the facts, how different versions of a tale may grow up.

The brevity of Old Irish Tales has always puzzled scholars when they contrast them with the verbose creations of early modern Irish, and Stephens had his own theories about the matter. *Irish Fairy Tales* attempts some unity through the presence of Finnen of Moville who listens eagerly to the first and last stories of the book, for though these are pagan, like Stephens, Finnen loves a good story. In 'Mongan's Frenzy', the abbot of the Monastery of Moville sends word to the story-tellers of Ireland to call at his monastery when they are near it, so that he may record the tales before they may die out, for 'it would be a pity if the people who come after us should be ignorant of what happened long ago, and of the deeds of their fathers,' he said. Cairidè, the descendant of Mongan's bard, comes and relates the story which has been passed down in his family:

> Vellum was then brought and quills. The copyists sat at their tables. Ale was placed beside the story-teller, and he told this tale to the abbot.

After this description of how the old tales were taken down from the oral account, and thus were notes, rather than complete compositions we are shown the attitude of the typical story-teller. The abbot objects to the part of the story where Tibraidè, a cleric, is ill-treated by Mongan.

Cairidè agreed that it was ill-done, but to himself he said gleefully that whenever he was asked to tell the story of how he told the story of Mongan he would remember what the abbot said.

Cairidè too shows earlier how tenaciously a seanachaidhe would cling to his own version of an event.

While in Paris in 1920 Stephens met B. W. Huebsch, the American publisher, who was the first to bring out *The Portrait of the Artist* in book form, to discuss his five volume epic. Stephens had completed the first two volumes, but, he wrote to Huebsch:

> I have, unfortunately, left Dublin for a month, & am unable to let you have the ms. you ask for. I am not yet prepared to publish as I do not wish the first volume to appear until three complete books of the sequence are finished, so that there would be no delay in keeping the pot boiling—as the children say & the publication of the five books would follow each other with sufficient regularity. The English Macmillans wish me to let them have both copyrights, but I do not wish to do this & am holding the matter over.

The following year, however, in February, he wrote to Huebsch again:

> You may remember our interview in Paris in late September of last year on the subject of my two stories, *The Land of the Young*, and *Deirdre*. These stories were left with your firm by my friend Mr. E. Boyd, late of this city. I have decided not to publish these stories for some time, and will be very much obliged if you will hand the mss. to Mr. John Quinn, 31 Massau Street, New York, to whom this letter is being sent.

After some further hesitation he published *Deirdre* and *In the Land of Youth*, both with Macmillans, in 1923 and 1924, perhaps realizing that the other three volumes were no further advanced and never would be.

Deirdre is the least successful of Stephens's recreations of Old Irish saga. It is the story beloved by the Anglo-Irish writers, more romantic than that of Diarmaid and Gránia, because Deirdre was a hounded martyr of fate, promised when an infant as wife to the High King of Ireland, whose pride made him believe that he could overcome the prophecy connecting her

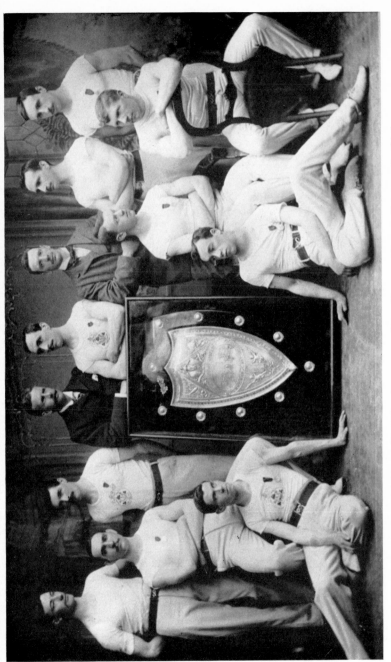

The Irish Shield, 1901. Winning team: The Dawson Street Gymnastic Club. (Stephens is seated on the ground, bottom right, and Tom Collins is on the end chair on the right, second row.)

James Stephens in middle age.

Woodside, the cottage and chapel near Cirencester.

with doom. Before the wedding she fled with Naoise and they spent seven idyllic years in Scotland together with his handsome brothers. Conchobair then sent Fergus to bring them back to Ireland and by a trick caused the death of the young men in order that he might marry Deirdre himself; but he was thwarted, for Deirdre, when she saw her lover and his brothers lying dead, died of grief.

Stephens gave a fine picture of life in early Celtic times for he turned to other sources when describing Conachúr's palace, finding full, if idealized, references to the appearances of royal houses in *Táin Bó Fraích* and *Tochmarc Emire*. His interest in Professor MacAlister's archaeological researches was also rewarding and he built up an authentic background to the narrative. The same attention to details of events remarkable in his other books is to be found. But treating the tale as a psychological novel upsets the movement of the first part. Analysis of the motives and characters of individuals provides great interest and gives breadth to the story but it slows up the action; and in the end he baulked the most important part of the tale, the flight of the lovers, and had it reported second-hand. It ends on a rather unfortunate chapter where Lavarcham has hysterics because her plans for Conachúr's marriage have all been shattered. Book two, however, is delightful and profits from the revelation of character in the first part. Perhaps the fact that in the original texts the greater part of the incidents occur after the flight may have caused Stephens's uncertainty as to how to treat the childhood of Deirdre. But the suppressed tragedy in the gaiety of Naoise's younger brothers, while Deirdre realizes that Conachúr's supposed friendship is treacherous, could not have been more successful. The end of the tale is good too, holding more power in its brevity than do the long drawn out versions of other writers.

In *Deirdre* Stephens was not interested in ideal beauty, and did not attach symbolic importance to it. He wanted to recapture the wonder of first love, the difficult situation of a girl placed between a man of her own age, and with her own experience of life, and a man who commands all her respect, but whose standing defies intimacy. It is amazing how he resurrected characters portrayed eight hundred years before and made them real for his own time: Fergus the gentle and

H

aristocratic king, brought to downfall through laziness; Conachúr with his 'warring mind', who gained the throne though a
trick and is persecuted by his sense of insecurity; the carefree
sons of Usnech, each different in character, and yet devoted to
one another; and Deirdre, herself, passionate, intuitive, and yet
driven from any measure of happiness by a relentless fate.

In all his treatment of Irish literature the equipment of a
natural sense of humour, and the affinity of his speech with
Irish diction, were greatly to Stephens's advantage. The ancient
legends of Ireland are distinctive for the marked individuality
of the characters and the detached humour the heroes display
when faced with the most terrifying situations. Stephens caught
this in his account of how Ardan and Ainnle go to their death;
but it was a natural gift, already apparent in *The Crock of Gold*:

> 'There's not much fun in being dead, sir,' said Meehawl.
> 'How do you know?' said the Philosopher.
> 'I know well enough,' replied Meehawl.

The general method of narration there is gently humorous and
is varied by the maxims of the Philosophers and their wives; the
accumulation of wisdom which the Philosopher pours out
indiscriminately; and in other places the juxtaposition of serious
and trivial. *The Demi-Gods* depends more on a general Irish
tradition of not taking life too seriously, and the conversation
consists of a form of Irish speech so slightly exaggerated as to
give it a tinge of humour. He was fortunate that his prose style
took what was best of the native expression and did not leave
the realms of probability as did Synge's. In *The Demi-Gods* and
in certain places in *The Crock of Gold* he appears to have been
parodying Synge's poetic lilt and cadence:

> Let you put your wings aside and your fine high crowns the way
> folk won't be staring at you every foot of the road, for I'm telling
> you that it's a bad thing to have people looking after you when
> you go through a little village or a town because you can never
> know who'll remember you afterwards, and you maybe not
> wanting to be remembered at all.

In the Grey Woman of Dun Gortin's lament for her husband,
he imitated Synge's 'waved' rhythm. Synge was the first to
equate the Irish *keen*, the formal wailing lamentation, with the
literary genre of English, and his lament of Deirdre has the

pauses, almost sobs and bursts of grief, of the traditional keen. Stephens never attempted a traditional keen. Following the instinct of his race to whom 'the half-said thing is dearest', he left Deirdre's grief to the imagination of his readers, and the only example is the parody in *The Crock of Gold*, where the bareness of the keen is reproduced to fine excess.

He treated *In the Land of Youth*, published in 1924, as two separate books, linked only by Maeve and her companions and the pending Táin. Part One consists of *Ectra Nera* (which provides a frame for the book), 'The Begetting of the Two Swineherds', and *Aislinge Œnguso*.[1] All are analyzed in Nutt's essay on the doctrine of rebirth which Stephens studied closely, and to which, as to Lady Gregory's books, he owed a great deal of his familiarity with the Celtic legends and heroes. Nera goes out for a wager on the Feast of Samhain (November), a time when it was customary to remain indoors to avoid the Shí, and when he returns finds that Cruachan has been sacked and all his companions scattered or killed. He alone is spared as he had been affected by the atmosphere of magic pervading the air on Samhain and has become a member of the Shí. He accepts his new life and settles down as servant and companion to a beautiful girl, who becomes his lover. In conversation between fairy and mortal Stephens worked out part of a philosophy applicable to our own life. The Shí may obtain whatever they want by wishing a disciplined wish; nothing may be desired that belongs to another person as then two wishes conflict; all desire must be pure and for necessities, such as contentment, good food and health, and so on and then one's wish will be fulfilled. Nera's fairy companion lives a simple life in Spartan conditions, but, as she says, having originally come from the human world, she has found her new life more than satisfying and there is nothing more that she can desire. Nera experiments with this idea, but he discovers before he begins that he does not know what he desires. When he has formed an image in his mind another image takes the place of his first desire before he has sufficiently concentrated on it to achieve his object. Eventually he realizes that his ultimate desire is that things should be as they were before he entered the fairy world

[1] *The Voyage of Bran and The Celtic Doctrine of Rebirth*, by Kuno Meyer and Alfred Nutt (2 vols.), London, 1895 and 1897.

and that Cruachan and its inmates should be restored. Different planes of existence are then revealed to him, worlds ennumerated in Old Irish mythology and here adapted by Stephens as a philosophic motif; this World of the Shí represents the first world of the mind where wishes may be fulfilled, and in fact the Sacking of Cruachan which Nera had seen had been Ethal Anbual, the King of the Fairies's, wish achieved in his world; but in the human world it had not come to pass at all. Time also differs in the two worlds and though he has spent three days with the Shí this is equivalent to three minutes in Cruachan where it is still Samhain, so he returns to his own people in order to warn them of Ethal Anbual's wish.

The story of Nera's journey into the Shí, his coming out to warn Maeve of Ethal Anbual's plan to attack Cruachan, and his electing to return to Faery where his love is, has the straightforward simplicity of the original text, but in fact Nera leaves the Fairy mound three times in the heroic tale. Stephens avoided confusion by this alteration, and the added leisure gives Maeve time to explain that the King of the Shí wishes to revenge himself on her because she sacked the Shí of Cruachan in order to get his daughter for Angus Óg, and to tell the origin of the bulls she stole from him then.

The second part of the book is devoted to another of the rémscela to the *Táin*, again told by Maeve, how Midir of the Shí won his wife back from the High King of Tara. Interruptions, though rather tedious, help to trace the complicated mythological relationships and the tale as a whole gives some impression of the writer's interest in reincarnation. The tales are interwoven most skilfully, and, as in *Deirdre*, Stephens's knowledge of the intricate relationships of his characters and the ease with which he shaped them into coherence for those to whom they were new is startling.

It was clearly his intention to keep these explanatory rémscela subordinate to the main *Táin* (which he never in fact published) for *Aislinge Œnguso* is abandoned before the uniting o Œngus with Caer, his dream love, and ends with Maeve removing the bulls from Faery. He deviated from the original account in which the vision of Caer appears to Œngus every night for a year, and confined it to one single occasion; and he improved his own story with a description typically his own of the most beautiful women in Ireland, and the delight they give to those who gaze on them. In the middle of the Œngus tale he interpolated the story of Friuc and Riuc, the two swineherds, who after various transformations become the Whitehorn and the Brown Bull, the subjects of the Táin saga. The Friuc and Riuc story is dealt with briefly, the author turning to the concise Book of Leinster version, for it must not cut into the main narrative too much; but this did not prevent him revelling in an account of the hunger of the pigs, which he dwelt on with joy and gusto.

The second part of *In The Land of Youth* is connected with the first through his own invention, for he decided to make the important events happen on the Feast of Lughnasa (August), another Fairy Festival. The temporary suspension of disbelief which these days require lifts the events out of ordinary life to the realm of enchantment and gives more room for imaginative creation. He treated a single tale, *Tochmarc Étaíne*, or the Wooing of Étain, and attempted to make a coherent whole out of the three fragments that have come down to us. The characters who are to be involved in the Táin interrupt the beginnings of the story with comments of their own, and so increase our knowledge of their background; and contrasting Étain and Maeve, while giving credence to Stephens's idea of the former, make us understand the fiery Queen better. Cuchulain, the heroic warrior, does not seem to have attracted Stephens much at all. He plays a very minor part in *Deirdre*, appearing as an overgrown schoolboy; and it is the more human characters such as Conachúr and Maeve whose weaknesses and interests are traced.

Stephens arranged the incidents narrated in the three fragments in a satisfactory way, making few alterations, but omitting what was unnecessary. There is an isolated incident in the first part where a horseman rides past the bathing maidens and gazes at Étain. It is undoubtedly Midir, the husband of her previous existence. But in Stephens's version it is Eochaid who finds Étain on the bank after her bathe, and it is then that he falls in love with her and marries her. At the end of the story, Midir claims Étain for his wife, instead of merely claiming a kiss, as in the text; and the omission of his name, when we know well who he is, with the sinister reference to the stranger, contribute to a vivid and exciting tale. In another part Étain has arranged to meet Ailill in the hut, and there is a clever description of her growing impatience, bad temper and guilt when he does not appear. But if Stephens had followed the original which causes Midir to appear three times instead of once, as in his version, this dramatic opportunity would have been lost. Stephens's arrangement and interpretation of the story justify Étain's behaviour to us in a way which a more accurate reproduction of the material could not have done, and the account of Midir's return and the abduction of Étain are developed so magnificently that Stephens himself is completely carried away and forgets who is telling the tale, and why it was begun.

In 1923 Stephens had won the Taillteann Gold Medal for *Deirdre*, and the following year he and A.E. were chosen to act as judges in the poetry section of the Taillteann Games, a festival for arts, literature and sports. His standing in his native country was assured. Yet, at the end of 1924, he resigned his post in the National Gallery and in 1925 he left Ireland, except for a few fleeting return visits, for ever. After this he wrote practically nothing at all; to leave his country where traditional tales had provided fresh themes for him was fatal.

The exact reason for his resignation from the National Gallery at this point is unknown. He had been offered a lecture tour in America and after contemplating a temporary absence he may have decided that he could now afford to live without a regular income. The job, it is true, overwhelmed him and left him little time for his own more important work. Perhaps he had never really believed that his epic would number five volumes, and he wished to explore the likelihood of a new way of writing. The thought of untrod ground in a new country may have excited him. Whatever the reason, he did not find it difficult to go, for the atmosphere of the New State was not to his taste and the dignity of the literary world of the early years of the century had declined. 'A world of job and jobbers has appeared,' he wrote to his friend, W. T. H. Howe, of the American Book Company, in June 1923, 'and the late gun-men are nowhere, or are wondering what it was they gunned for anyway.' He saw a great future for Seán O'Casey; *The Shadow of a Gunman* had made a great impact on him, but he himself must go. After a lecture tour in America, his first, and a visit to Paris, he took a house outside Wembley near London, where he lived for the rest of his life. He told Justice Reddin that the Wembley Stadium would have some interest to him, and he attempted to cover his regret at the voluntary exile with a joke: 'The only people that read me in the world live in the little houses in Wembley.'

PART TWO

London — 1925 - 1950

—I would think
Until I found
Something
I can never find;
—Something
Lying
On the ground
In the bottom
Of my mind.
    The Goat-Paths

VII

London

We are at the beginning of an era, and who creates a new
world must create a new art to express it!
Preface to Collected Poems

LIFE in London was a complete change for Stephens. Stephen
MacKenna had also left Ireland and was settled in Bourne-
mouth, so he was able to visit him often, usually staying for
about ten days at a time. MacKenna used to insist on him
accompanying him on Sundays to Mass for old time's sake.
They resumed the long conversations of former days and
strummed on their guitars again in MacKenna's tiny cottage,
which was lined with books, musical instruments and rows of
Buddhas. (MacKenna would buy Buddhas wherever he went,
and soon the garden too was full of them). 'For tone he's a
jewel,' wrote MacKenna in appreciation of Stephens's guitar
playing—'a rambling meditativeness, a subtlety of summer
breezes, a vision of a vague Heaven (the kind Heavens do be);
also he sometimes talks.'[1]

Glimpses of A.E. were brief, for A.E. disliked England, and
apart from Colum, all news of other friends was secondhand.
From time to time his longing to see Dublin was so great that
Stephens would slip over to the city for a weekend; and he
would visit the mountains nostalgically too. In Summer 1930,
he stayed in the Arts Club and appeared at a party Lennox
Robinson gave at his cottage at Sorrento in Dalkey. His stories
and the way he related them that evening have become legend:
the story of the primadonna who used to gargle with cold cream
to preserve her voice and gargled with secotine by mistake one
night, thereby causing her vowels to stick to the consonants and
come out in lumps; and stories of his childhood. As a boy, he

[1] *Journal and Letters of Stephen MacKenna*, p. 280. Edited with a memoir by
E. R. Dodds, London, 1936.

said, he and his friends made a raid on a fruit stall, attracted by some bright red fruit they had never seen before. A policeman giving chase had nearly caught him and he crammed the fruit into his mouth in order to hide it, but the curious flavour took him completely by surprise and he remained rooted to the ground in astonishment and took the beating without a word. In a more flippant mood he told how he and a friend were travelling in a railway carriage to Bray when an old gentleman climbed in and how they spent the rest of the journey daring each other to speak to him. 'Please, sir,' blurted out Stephens just before they left the train, 'Is the next station the one after this?' He acted his next story, a story about Paris, where he had dinner one evening with a young couple who were newly married and to whom he presented a cigarette lighter. To murmurs of admiration the lighter travelled round the room, from hand to hand, until it reached Stephens, who nonchalantly replaced it in his pocket. (He gave it back to them later.)

In the winter of 1931–2 he returned to Dublin to give a poetry recital in the Abbey Theatre which was a great success. Afterwards he and A.E. lamented the contemporary trend of life and the increasing predominance of internal combustion engines and machinery in a world where bushes, trees, insects and animals were of greater importance. Stephens then became confidential about the change in England, and admitted that when talking to the English he felt himself sucked of stories, like a jug that had been turned upside down, and he considered that the absence of repartee in conversation was responsible for this. He was back to his old form that night however, and entertained every one near him to a performance of an oriental dance, where he sat crosslegged and motionless on a sofa. With hands folded he closed his eyes. Then he opened them and looked to the left, without moving his head. The next step was to look to the right, and then he demonstrated the climax, the shifting of the eyes to their original position when they looked forward into space once more.

In the early part of 1935 he stayed longer in Dublin. Joseph Hone had taken a house, Southill, in Killiney, for six months while writing his book on George Moore; and every Thursday evening expected his literary friends. Even during the railway strike the house was full. Conversation turned in the main on

George Moore and his books. Stephens was his old charming self, likening himself to Voltaire who believed he most closely resembled a monkey; and he sustained the whole room as an audience with his brilliant conversation. However in general visits were short and infrequent. 'I should love to go over again to Dublin, but poetry gets one from this address to Piccadilly Circus and back again,' Stephens wrote to Mrs. Bodkin in 1939 when she wrote to congratulate him on *Kings and the Moon*.

It was not long before he found himself firmly accepted in London literary circles, and though he missed the evenings in Dublin, the great admiration his charm won everywhere must have pleased him, and he experienced more intellectual stimulus than he was to find in America. At Lady Ottoline Morrell's house he and Yeats held the floor, arguing for hours about Irish politics. Here he met Dilys Powell and they quickly became friends. The young writer appreciated his sympathy and used to offer her early verses to Stephens for criticism. He used to visit Miss Powell for afternoon tea. 'His deeply-lined face, broad above and narrow below, sat on a little neck under an Irish tweed tinker's hat,' she remembers. He talked about his youth in a romancing manner, and about his prowess as an athlete; and he was generous beyond measure with his money, pouring it out on presents for everyone. In particular he had an eye for trinkets and jewellery, but his wife had to keep a firm hand on the purse strings because he never could keep money. Miss Powell found that Stephens had scarcely any small talk but headed straight for the subject of poetry and he adored repeating it as an incantation. He would sing at a certain tone-level, in a deep 'organ' voice, his eyes bright and fixed, his throat swelling. He felt passionately about cruelty—when repeating 'The Snare' he would be close to tears—and he used to refer with deep loathing to the time of the Black and Tans in Ireland. When not occupied talking he would be drawing humorous squiggles and outlines wherever he could.

He still visited Paris frequently, though for short periods, and continued to do so up to the end of his life, on the slightest pretext. 'He's flying last Saturday, so I suppose is flown, to Paris—for why do you suppose?' wrote MacKenna to Margaret Nunn,[1] in 1931:

[1] See footnote p. 111.

Because a Russian told him of a shop in Paris where music was
(is and will be) to be sold, arranged from the 7-string Russian
guitar for the Spanish and Ringwoodian 6-stringer: he has stax
of guitarities that no one could ever play . . .

James Joyce had become a friend of his. At their first meeting
in Dublin, according to Stephens, he and Joyce had not taken
to each other, but when he came to Paris Joyce sought to
renew their acquaintance and was very friendly. He later discovered that Joyce believed their birthdate was identical, the
second of February 1882, and since they were both called
James, and the name of Joyce's autobiographical hero 'Stephen'
was Stephens's name too, he superstitiously felt that their
friendship would hold some good portent. In 1913 Stephens
had told Bodkin in a letter that he thought Joyce would be a
better writer if he were more natural and in a letter to W. T. H.
Howe on 24 April 1917, he said Joyce was 'a disappointed,
envious man'; but now as he grew to understand him his
opinion altered. The two men had something in common
besides their mutual love of literature. In fact the latter interest
may not have been a happy link since Joyce's scholarly mind
must have clashed with Stephens's intuitive and emotional
approach, and the choice of James Stephens to finish *Finnegan's
Wake* was surely not a serious intention on the part of Joyce.
But both writers were fond of folk songs and used to sing them
to one another. 'The Brown and Yellow Ale', which Stephens
later sang in a broadcast, was said to have come from the
midlands of Ireland:

> I was walking the road one fine day
> —O the Brown and the Yellow Ale—
> When I met a man was no right man
>   O Love of my Heart
>
> And he asked if the woman with me was my daughter
> —O the Brown and the Yellow Ale—
> And I said she was my married wife
>   O Love of my Heart
>
> And he asked me would I lend her for an hour and a quarter
> —O the Brown and the Yellow Ale—
> And I said I would do anything that was fair
>   O Love of my Heart

So you take the high road and I'll take the lower
—O the Brown and the Yellow Ale—
And we'll meet again at the ford of the river
 O Love of my Heart

I was waiting there for a day and a quarter
—O the Brown and the Yellow Ale—
When she came to me without any shame
 O Love of my Heart

When I heard her tale I lay down and I died
—O the Brown and the Yellow Ale—
And she sent two men to the woods for timber
 O Love of my Heart

A board of holly and a board of elder
—O the Brown and the Yellow Ale—
And two great yards of sacking about me
 O Love of my Heart

And if it wasn't that my own little mother was a woman
—O the Brown and the Yellow Ale—
I'd sing another pretty song about women
 O Love of my Heart

This song Stephens claimed to have heard from no one but Joyce.

He composed a poem for Joyce's birthday, which he included in *Strict Joy* under the name 'Sarasvati', the Hindu name for the mind of the Demiurgic Creator, and the name of the goddess of hidden wisdom (he would have taken this from Madame Blavatsky's *The Secret Doctrine*). Joyce and he became very close in some strange manner; and his final view, expressed in a broadcast, was very different from his first opinion; 'Joyce went straight for the truth and wrote what he felt.'

He met many eminent people at Lady Ottoline Morrell's house in London on Thursday afternoons, Augustus John, Lytton Strachey, Douglas Brown, W. J. Turner, Middleton Murry, and Leonard Woolf, among others, and they were frequent visitors at his own home. The younger poets, who took life seriously, such as Stephen Spender, did not like Stephens at all.

By far the closest friendship he formed was with Koteliansky, the big Russian Jew, and it was a lasting friendship, for 'Kot' felt protective towards Stephens, perhaps sensing a kinship in the mystic idealism natural to them both. Stephens experienced a beneficial influence in this relationship because their basic views and beliefs were identical and Kot, a leader, helped him to more definite opinions on outside affairs. Once Lady Glenavy asked Kot how he liked the thought of being completely taken in by James's leprechaun act, as all the non-Irish were; and Kot replied in a reproving manner that astonished by its vehemence, 'Under that leprechaun façade is a real suffering human'.

Samuel Solomonovitch Koteliansky had emigrated from the Russian Ukraine before the First World War in order to research into Economics at London University and had then taken a job at the Russian Law Bureau, which he hated. He was a reader at the Cresset Press for a number of years. He was a natural critic with a sixth sense for good literature and excellent judgement, but in the end this critical faculty was his undoing, because he tended to choose books that were excellent literature but which did not sell easily, so the Cresset Press pensioned him off. Nobody knew how Kot lived on the tiny pension. His one extravagance was a particular kind of tobacco which he bought in a Jewish shop in the East End of London, even during the War. He would roll his own cigarettes, and he and Stephens would smoke them as they talked.

Kot was proud, a despot and according to Leonard Woolf the epitome of an Old Testament prophet. He was intensely loyal to the people he loved, who were few—D. H. Lawrence and Katherine Mansfield were among them—and those whom he disliked he would refer to as 'kriminal stinks'. There was usually no tangible reason for his likes and dislikes; he inclined to turn against the wife or husband of his dearest friends, through jealousy, no doubt, because his affection was so demanding and of a permanent nature. Every Thursday afternoon James Stephens would visit Kot at his flat in 5 Acacia Avenue. He would trot down the basement steps to the kitchen, always wearing the same disreputable mackintosh, and the same battered felt hat pulled down over his eyes. The coat hung loose on him, and the flesh drooped on the bones of his face, and the whole effect could have been of a man who was

depressed and dilapidated, had not he himself been so delight-
fully charming and gay. He would take off his coat and hat and
sit down, and he and Kot would talk together for hours, drinking pints of tea, with a certain ritual. Then Kot would prepare
a Martini with special herbs added and after two or three
glasses Stephens would shut his eyes and rock backward and
forward, reciting his poems in a crooning voice, while Kot's
eyes beamed behind the horn-rimmed spectacles and he sat
straight on his hard deal chair. May Sarton has left a picture
of a typical afternoon in Koteliansky's flat in her autobiography:

> Kot is sitting at the kitchen table, pronouncing 'In the hierarchy
> of creation there is God Almighty and Leo Tolstoy'; Lawrence
> is putting a duck in the oven; K.M. is writing at her table in the
> upper room;[1] James is drinking gin and crooning poems; and
> down at the end of the garden the pear tree is in flower.

No one might interrupt or join the conversation when Stephens
and Kot were in full flow. Diatribes on every subject came from
Stephens; and literary topics in particular occupied them.
Lady Huxley remembers them discussing T. S. Eliot. They had
a strange affinity in their attitude to life. 'They were both, from
our point of view,' writes Ruth Pitter,

> exotics. James did not know, he said, where he was born
> (? professional Irishman's apocryphal statement) and Kot
> certainly did not know *when* he was born; he said that around
> Kiev at that time they only remembered such things by the
> season; he also related that being pastoral people, and the
> summer very hot, the milk was sour by the time they got it
> home, and that the natives would have their winter felt stockings
> hung all round the eaves in summer; the sour milk was poured
> directly into these, the whey ran off, and fine leg-shaped cheeses
> were the final result. James might then recall that food in any
> form was desirable, and often hard to get, and then he remem-
> bered wrenching half a muddy loaf from the jaws of an immense
> stray dog, and forcing it to share with him. Cold was an enemy
> as bad as hunger; he had been a feeble infant, and remembered
> his mother, or at least some woman, frequently feeling his feet,
> and if they were chill, she would drop everything and rush in to

[1] If this is Katherine Mansfield she was there only in spirit as she died
in 1923.

bed with him until he warmed up. These tales used to strike me as sounding as though they had been translated from some Balkan language; their roots were elsewhere, though the themes were so universal.

Buried in conversation, they would hear, at about half-past five, Mrs. Stephens's car-horn honking outside and Stephens would stop talking, jump up and hustle on his coat and hat. No one could persuade him to stay. He couldn't wait, he would say; he was late already and then he rushed away. On one occasion Lady Glenavy listened to a long discussion covering the whole range of English literature. At the end Stephens turned to her and said, 'the greatest book on literature that has never been written is by Koteliansky'.

Kot and Stephens would also meet at Twinings in Piccadilly. They would go to dinner afterwards in Great Portland Street and end the evening in the Casa Prada, near Warren Street. Another favourite haunt was Ridgeway's where it soon became a habit to meet on Wednesdays, and a group formed including Ralph Hodgson, Leonard Woolf, J. W. N. Sullivan, Lady Glenavy, sometimes Mark Gertler or W. J. Turner, Lady Ottoline Morrell, Middleton Murry and Lady Huxley. Poetic discussion was lively, and Stephens would often scribble out one of his poems on a piece of paper and give it to Kot, who preserved several among his papers;

> It has been writ in wisdom old
> That this is the last word to be told;
> There is no Dissolution, no Creation,
> There are none in woe:
> There is no Teacher, Teaching, Taught:
> And none who long for, lack for aught:
> Are none who pine for freedom,
> None liberated under sun:
> And this is absolutely true,
> In Him who dreams in Me and You.[1]

These meetings ceased during the Blitz, but there had been marvellous talk there, about poetry and poets. Lady Huxley once mentioned a poem of Gerard Manley Hopkins's which was too complex for her. Stephens asked her for the book, and read the poem aloud, making it lucid and meaningful. He used

[1] Among Stephens's letters to Kot in the British Museum.

to relate stories by acting them. He told one about a bee which flew into his greenhouse, and he enacted its buzzing in the sunlight, and the wicked menacing spider crouching in its web in the corner, with the final struggles of the bee as it was caught. He was full of vivid tales about animals. Dr. Monk Gibbon remembers him expatiating on the loves of the spiders on his wooden garden fence at Wembley, as viewed from afar by a benevolent deity in the shape of his garden tortoise. He used to say that he went into the garden to talk with the trees and one evening in his enthusiasm, describing a bush spreading upward from the ground, covered with pink flowers, worked himself into an ecstasy as he explained how he had attempted to become one with that bush.

While he swiftly established an oral reputation for himself in London, Stephens found that he wrote less and less, and he tended to rework old material; what writing he did was now concerned solely with mystic subjects. In June 1925, shortly after he had left Dublin, he published *A Poetry Recital*, the poems used on his American tour, which included pieces from *Songs From the Clay*, and *The Adventures of Seumas Beg*; and here appeared the first poems in his new style. The old rambling conversational tone was abandoned as he concentrated himself in communion with the All-Being and advocated loneliness; and this inspired dedication lent itself to a tense method of expression, which did not permit him to glance about on each side in his former leisurely manner, and which robbed his vocabulary of his fluency.

The following year, in 1926, he published his *Collected Poems*, drawing from all his volumes, including *A Poetry Recital* and *Little Things*, which had come out in America in 1924.

He had always revised his poems, sometimes changing only an odd word, and at other times rewriting whole sentences. This had happened especially with certain *Seumas Beg* poems, when they appeared in *The Adventures of Seumas Beg*, five or more years after they were first composed, but in *Collected Poems* there was a general revision of verse forms and punctuation. This was because of the recitals of his work which he was giving more and more frequently. His verse had always been oral, but now it became consciously so, and he wished to express this quality in writing. In *A Poetry Recital* he had given instructions for the method of reading some of the poems. Now with his old poems he broke up long lines into two or more short ones, he added exclamation marks in abundance, dashes in place of inverted commas, and triplicate dots to give more force to sentences and single words. The shorter lines also emphasize words by isolating them and giving them more length of sound, and these features were characteristic of any verse written after this date. Importance was now to be placed in the single word.

'The Goat Paths' in its new form simulated a winding path, but:

> By a hidden beaten way,

which suggested the trod of goat hooves, was altered to:

> All among
> The heather spray.

This is more remote and does not break the delicacy of mood of the dreaming poet; for, in this version, the final and rather mystical stanza seemed more important to the poet than the movements of goats which intrigued him when the poem was first written.

Other poems were broken up into triplets or couplets, because he felt that his early verse had tumbled over itself, and that the new frame gave more significance to each phrase, where an impression had previously been sufficient. Lines were changed and verses often omitted, which was sometimes an improvement; however the beauty of the poem and its impish humour are totally lost in the new version of 'The Satyr'.

'The Holy Time' differs almost completely, both in wording and in structure from the 1915 version but in the change of

> And now the dusk of evening draws upon
> That memory of light,
> And light is gone!

when trying to be more exact, Stephens in fact caused confusion because the impression he wanted to describe was not general enough and seems vague to those who have not had similar experiences. This is the difficulty with his mystic poems and it has led to the criticism that they are obscure.

Collected Poems is divided into six parts, each embodying a different mood, and grouped together in this way the predominance of mystic poems is immediately apparent. Significantly 'The Goat Paths' was chosen to open the volume. In Section One, 'In Green Ways', the link of man and nature is felt deeply; and 'A Honeycomb' groups love poems and those depicting a struggle between the sexes. The poems of 'In The Two Lights' move from the gentle depression and healing rest of dusk to stark winter verses, but a hopeful note is struck in the final poem, 'Christmas At Freelands', where the snow laden air sings that 'all we love is born again'. The following section gives a respite from serious thought, and Stephens also excused the radical element of his early poems in the jovial title 'Heels over Head', so toning down the boisterous poems which attacked the God of established Christianity, and the naïvité of the Seumas Beg poems. 'Less Than Daintily' continues in similar strain, with the remaining poems from *Insurrections* and the more robust outbursts in *Reincarnations* which called mankind to love and sympathy; but 'What's the Use' was placed at the end of the section because the sixth part was to pose his final peaceful solution. Joy is 'The Golden Bird', which is bird and flesh but is utterly free. Turning from the first poems in this last section, poems written at the beginning of his career which showed that man could not be master of situation, Stephens revealed in the first examples of his new verse that the answer is experience and complete acceptance of every aspect of existence, and he concluded the collection with the words:

> What is Knowing?
> 'Tis to see!
> What is Feeling?
> 'Tis to be!
> What is Love? But, more and more,
> To See and Be! To be a Pour
> And Avalanche of Being, till
> Being ceases, and is still
> For every motion—What is Joy?
> —Being, past all earthly cloy
> And intermixture! Being spun
> Of Itself is Being won!
> That is Joy—And this is God,
> To be That, in cloud and clod:
> And, in cloud and clod, to sing
> Of Everything, and Anything!

VIII

The Final Philosophy

Imagination does but seem:
Thought is wisdom, in a dream.
                    Demiurge

IN 1928 Stephens published *Etched in Moonlight*, a collection of short stories, some of which had already appeared in periodicals. 'Hunger' (1918) was included among them. He had always been interested in problems of relationships, in families, between friends, and between friend and enemy, and in those of a wider and spiritual nature. In *The Demi-Gods*, for instance, he inserted among the medley of interpretations of the creation of man and comments on his way of life, the tale of two people who have never given anything of themselves to each other. The man has buried himself in his books and curiosities, the woman is secretive and unyielding; and though there is a moment at which they are given the opportunity to reach each other, neither is willing to take the initial step and it is clear that they cannot remain together. He played with situations such as this in a detached manner, intrigued with the incompatibilities of personality yet essaying no solution, for disparity of affection is basic to complex civilization. Formalities arising from human encounter too were fascinating to him. 'There can be nothing more uncomely,' said the first angel, 'than to see people acting in disaccord with custom.'

Reality, its nature and extent, however, puzzled him and this was a matter he probed deeply.

Art thou done
Thou winged one?
Then whither dost thou fly
Or where
Seeing there is no anywhere

122

Seeing there is no anyone
Who would be come or gone
Why dost thou spread a wing
In air
Who art not anything
Or anywhere

he pencilled in the back of *Essays in Zen Buddhism,* by D. T. Suzuki, one of the books on Eastern religion he studied during the 'twenties. Time was elusive and could be nothing but illusion. 'There is no time, there is but consciousness and its experiences,' he decided, and he tried to achieve the effect of what our consciousness registers in several short stories. 'Sawdust', published in *The Century Magazine* in 1918, describes a dipsomaniac who sits in a public house haunted by memories of the past and unaware of what is happening about her. She is suspended in her own mood and thus utterly withdrawn. A priest comes in to the public house to chastise the drinking women; his words break through to her with a jolt, bringing her face to face with herself, and she instantly leaves. Later they find that she has drowned herself. The effect of the fair on 'The Wolf', published at the same time, is also interesting:

> The world was there before him. A world of squawks and squeals and grunts and cackles and shrill calls of women and great guffaws of men, with now and then the long lamentable uproar that is made by a donkey, pealing above all other noises, and continually the sharp and gruff and eager bark, yelp, howl, growl, and snarl of every kind of dog that you could put a name to. At a little distance all these noises became one sound, and it is the sound of the sea.
>
> He heard that sound and he walked into it; it swallowed him up, and therein he disappeared from mortal eye for six years.
>
> When he reappeared, the sun was sinking in a red distance; the fair was all gone home again; there was deep silence everywhere, and he was as drunk as a lord.

The time he spent at the fair is exaggerated since it depicts a few hours of emancipation from a hectoring wife, life as he wished to live it permanently. The fallaciousness of time as a measure is illustrated in *In The Land of Youth*, where Nera's three days in Faery represent barely three minutes of human time.

Since outside influences so dominate our consciousness, perhaps then we are utterly dependent on other mortals and on places for existence? Eochaid, for example, when he senses the withdrawal of the love of God and of his people's loyalty, feels he is no man but a mere shell. Natural phenomena, too, were not exempt from these modulations and in his poetry he inspected silence and its relation to noise, and the grades of darkness that may be distinguished at night. This led to man's connection with natural phenomena and the various effects contributing to the growth of his emotions. Our experience is not based on our actions, but on what we are, he observed in *Irish Fairy Tales;* for we may easily participate in an event without feeling that we are present at all. In fact we do not go to Faery, or to the happy state, we become Faery. He finally found the solution to problems of reality in dream and sleep, and this after some study of Freud, and, more important, Indian philosophy. He defined three conditions of being—waking, dreaming and deep-sleep; all of these are 'actual', or seem to exist, but only the last is 'real'. It is the 'Everywhere', and the Being who is there is the 'Everyone'.

He analyzed dream, the lightning speed of dream and the fantastic powers automatically assumed through the medium of dreams. The events of the short story 'Etched in Moonlight' take place in a dream so that emotions and gestures will be especially significant, for Stephens wished to experiment with the symbolism of Yeats's 'system'; the story is a failure, however, because Yeats's system was too complex for him. There are three friends, two men and a woman, who are divided when the woman falls in love with one of them. The other is smitten with jealousy; and Stephens describes his changing moods of affection, hatred, regret and terror during the course of the relationship. He even hopes to kill the lovers by immuring them in an old castle, but they escape after a few moments. Years later, he himself is closed into the castle, but unlike them, he cannot find his way out of the dungeon which separates him from the Moon, or light and inspiration. The Moon is also complete subjectivity and its antithesis is complete annihilation of self. The central character is unaware at what phase of the

Moon his will lies and we, too, are only half aware of the effect
of the dark of the moon until the end, when we are shown his
'wire-jointed jaws and limbs of wood'. But Stephens is certain
of the radiant joy that fills anyone whose self is blotted out in
this manner even if, as in this case, his existence is terminated.
The mad man has become unbelievably happy. All memory of
the past has been erased and he is irradiated with contentment.

Buddhism, or the form of Buddhism that Stephens adopted,
justified the fellow-feeling he had for animals. Apart from a
genuine affection for other creatures, his dependence on the
stability in the course of Nature may be traced clearly in his
poetry. The tragic element of human life was a constant concern. Human transiency troubled him and the fact that our
oys and sorrows rely on other people who are as short-lived as
we. In Nature, however, the pattern of being never comes to
an end. Plants die in winter and are born again in spring.
Nature simply accepts what occurs, passively, and lives without
apprehensions, using the materials that are to hand. Our fears
and sorrows are of our own making; we are separate from other
people and can never join ourselves to them, so why should we
not adopt Nature's 'careless' attitude? If peace is to be found
we will find it within ourselves and nowhere else. The need to
develop such a philosophy was first expressed in 'The Goat
Paths' and he was sure that the goats had already found wisdom
in their 'sunny solitude'. Nature is free, he stated elsewhere,
because she has readily accepted her powers, weaknesses and
duties. Now man must demand her forgiveness because he has
split the unity of natural objects by his questionings. Men
rightly form part of the succession and movement of nature,
and are brothers of 'each bird and tree', and if the bonds of
daily life, the

> flat
> Dull catalogue of weighty things,

that have accrued and bound men down were rejected, natural
blessedness would be revived. The donkey in *The Demi-Gods* is
the analogue of Finaun, the eldest, most perfect angel, and is
both wise and kind. He has companions in all levels of life, the
Cyclops, who signify power, but are capable of tenderness, as
we see in their gentle treatment of the donkey, the fairy host,

who have achieved a more spiritual state than human beings, the maidens and the centaurs. The mystical numbers of seven and three in the groups of maidens and centaurs indicate blessedness. The centaurs, too, had a special attraction for Stephens because they are half human and half animal, and in classical mythology are credited with great wisdom. Nevertheless, when the donkey meets with his free brothers, the wild asses, and sees them triumph over sly men, his selflessness asserts itself and he declines their invitation to join them in their freedom, for he has a great affection for Mary MacCann, and feels a responsibility towards her.

Stephens never attached much importance to the Doctrine of Reincarnation as such. In 'Etched in Moonlight' reincarnation adds another dimension to the planes of reality. The dreamer is conscious that he was himself in the previous life; but he lived in a different time and place, with different conventions, and language, and knew different people, and all were as familiar to him as those he now knows. *Irish Fairy Tales* and *In The Land of Youth* treat two stories of rebirth, and in other places it is briefly referred to; but Stephens did not look on animals as reincarnations of fellow human beings. He believed that some beings are secure against the forces of evil, and live as by divine right because they deserve it. They attract good, and seethe 'with energy and innocence and all the animation of a budding life', while the evil man must receive the evil to which he is accustomed. This view refers directly to the Buddhist law of 'causation' in human nature, and is similar to Yeats's theory that mankind must complete certain cycles of being and thus strengthen itself before reaching perfection. Those whom Stephens referred to as 'old souls' were those who had acquired wisdom, and 'young souls' were those in need of further development.

Stephens did not concentrate on Indian philosophy because it provided a satisfactory explanation for existence; indeed he never looked for a reason for living; it was the character of being that demanded his attention. He sought peace through the training of the mind, and he found it in Yoga, in so far as he found it. Indian philosophy emphasizes a passive attitude towards life, which may be achieved by contemplation. There is more awareness than in Christianity of man's position in the natural order. Brahman, or God, is the universal Self, the one Reality, and is eternal peace; duality and friction are characteristics of Maya, illusion, which is the world we live in. Duality means that God and Man's spirit and God and Nature are not one and the same. The essence of Buddhist philosophy may be found in the Doctrine of Perfect Enlightenment. This teaches that man must realize the ultimate truth within himself and through his own efforts, before he may rid himself of illusion, for no one may reveal it to him; and Enlightenment is Nirvana, Nothingness, Brahman. 'Know life as a long sleep, and the world with myself and thyself are the visions of its dream. We see many other persons in this sleepy dream, none of whom is real.'[1] Brahman is also called Absolute Consciousness and he is to be reached through knowledge, which is the destruction of ignorance. Ignorance is caused by Desire, the attaching of oneself to transient objects. The man of Desire also concerns himself with the results of action, and this is the reason why, though good action may acquire a position from which one may win to Enlightenment in the next life, lack of action is more worthy, for it is beyond desire. To meditate on the eternal spirit leads to identification with the eternal spirit; and the man who sees this spirit in every creature attains immortal life. Man's mind forms the bridge between Maya and Brahman, but will is superior to mind and is the instrument by which knowledge may be acquired. Yoga, the exercise of the mind which joins man to God, teaches that the Self is the Seer, and the mind belongs to the seen, so that it is necessary for the disciple to purify his mind of all extraneous matter that it may reflect the Self. Austerity and self-control and meditation are the means of purification.

Buddhism, a reformed version of the original Hinduism, does not condemn other religions or ways of worship, but it teaches that self-discipline is more important than sacrifices and advises the Middle Way between indulgence and self-torture. The two cardinal virtues in Buddhism are wisdom, which one arrives at through knowledge, and love.

The tenets of Theosophy, Be-ness or Absolute Negation, and the human plane of Duality, gave Stephens a background to

[1] *The Yoga-Vasishtha-Maharamayana of Valmiki* by Vihari-Lala Mitra, Calcutta, 1891, Vol. I, p. 438.

Indian philosophic teaching, but dependence on astrology and the occult hindered him and it was not until he turned to the purer doctrines of Buddhism that he seriously occupied himself with the problem of reality. The latter's object is single; it has rejected the numerous gods of the older Hindu religion, and Stephens made use of Buddhist symbolism in only one place, where its significance is universal. Fire because of its cleansing quality is sacred to Buddhists, and Stephens's training of his mind is imaged in the title of the poem 'Student Taper'. He also studied Sankara, of a later date but with similar ideas to Buddhism, the Persian mystics, and Zen Buddhism, but the practicality of the last did not attract him as much as the speculative aphorisms of the Indians did. It was to Yoga and mind-discipline that he devoted most of his attention. In the latter part of his life he read little else.

Theme and Variations, the poem involved with Plotinus's teaching,[1] contains the first complete statement of Stephens's philosophy of life; elsewhere his ideas are incoherent or isolated, until the later poems.[2] 'Religion is self-consciousness,' he wrote in 1914, when he rejected the twisted Theology of orthodox Christianity; and in *The Demi-Gods* he equated love and knowledge, the two great tenets of Buddhism. An article in *The New Age* in 1913[3] showed that he knew the *Mahabarata*, which he later called, in one of his enthusiastic moods, the greatest book ever written. Yeats was sufficiently impressed to remark in his letters that Stephens had read the *Táin* in the light of the *Veda*, though this is perhaps a slight exaggeration, for Stephens did not devote himself to Indian philosophy to the exclusion of all else until the nineteen-twenties. But during the 'twenties he read and re-read the *Upanishads* and the *Bhagavad-gita*, and the commentaries on them, and he went to great trouble to obtain the four huge volumes of *The Yoga-Vasishtha-Maharamayana of Valmiki* by Vihari-Lala Mitra. All were thoroughly read and marked or annotated, and some of his verses were drafted roughly in the fly pages. His ideal of a 'calm and steadfast soul' propounded in 1908 was now to be achieved by stern discipline. Indeed Stephens separated the body and

---

[1] Composed in 1929. See Chapter IX.
[2] *Strict Joy*, 1931; *Kings and the Moon*, 1938.
[3] 'Enter Mr. James Stephens' (*The New Age*), 20 November 1913.

the ideal state of mysticism in a horrifying way in 'Away! Far
Away!' Life is Food and Darkness, while far away is all of spirit
and beauty. And in *Etched in Moonlight*, he described many
times the exhaustion that an untrained mind suffers when any
strain is put on it. Through practice, 'mind-binding' power is
attained:

> An hurricane of knowing, that
> Could whelm the soul that was not pat
> To flinch and lose the deadly thing.

Even grief, he noted in 'Strict Care, Strict Joy!' may be converted by discipline into joy.

The Will is our instrument. To will something is to cause it
to happen; for an act of will is an act of being, and it dispenses
with the mind. Still Stephens clung to the importance of
Imagination and believed that it, and not the mind, set the
Will to work; but Imagination was not the source of God. Nor
was wise Emotion, or Thought; for the Will, 'The Wide-Awake,
the Living Thing', was the Demiurge, the original creator of
the world in Platonic philosophy.

In 'Optimist' Stephens made it plain that we must live with
humanity until we achieve disciplined perfection and our mind
'grows wise and kindly'; and he counselled wise acceptance of
the ways of life, finding God, not in discussion with other men,
but in the quiet of the Moon. The Moon, for Yeats and
Stephens, symbolized the light of revelation; it is the opposite
of reason, which Stephens rejected as an approach to the
Infinite. Deirdre finds her love, Naoise, after surrendering
herself to the Moon, and a description of moonlight—the full
of the Moon—where all is one, shows its infinite holiness.

Stephens realized that this ultimate peace might be obtained
in one way only. Yoga teaches that our minds reject all else and
are unaffected by outside issues when they concentrate on a
single object. If we concentrate on Ultimate Reality, therefore,
it is from this that we will receive our inspiration. Even Love
must be rejected. In 'Thy Soul' Stephens used the story of
Nachiketas, from the *Katha Upanishad*, as a frame for his ideas,
but the exultation was all his own; Death alone can give us
knowledge, which is Bliss and Eternity. Then we shall return
to the Creator who is ourself: 'He is the Dreamer and the

Dream!' This is reminiscent of Yeats's 'How can we know the Dancer from the Dance?' Yeats, however, insisted that the body will be part of this final reality, while Stephens regarded the body as part of the illusion.

We may not achieve this blessed state of Nothingness until all desire has been annihilated. Desire, besides making a slave of us, is the cause of Illusion, our impermanent world; it is the equivalent of Ignorance, and yet more disastrous, for it has the power of Will in mortal form. What we desire we become, and an ill-considered desire may have fatal effects. The short story 'Desire' in *Etched in Moonlight* illustrates the evil in two ways. Stephens again used the curiously anonymous form of story-telling habitual in his short stories after he went to France, and it helped to isolate the point he wished to convey. In the story, a business man, crossing the road at lunch-time, pulls back another pedestrian from under a car. They fall into conversation and go off together for lunch, and they pass the time discussing religious matters. The stranger, in particular, is interested to hear what the other man would choose if he were granted a wish. The latter relates the event to his wife. Whereas the husband is aware of his comfortable position and secure future, the wife is attached to material wealth through her ungoverned desire. She cannot understand why her husband refused a chance of additional riches. At night, she dreams that she is on an Arctic expedition; this symbolizes the journey of life. She is equipped with all the warm clothing and gear she may need, but she puts off using them even when it grows unbearably cold. These are the faculties and gifts she had been provided with for her human life, but she prefers to hoard them and to delight solely in their possession. All talk on board centres round the baggage, the wordly goods we own. But the foolish woman, when forced by the intensity of the cold to turn to her clothing, finds that it has disappeared. The ship vanishes then—that is, her life ends, and she finds the other people who have used their possessions go on their journey and abandon her, while she is lost in a wilderness of frozen ice. When she awakes, she finds that her husband, whom she had probably never appreciated during his lifetime, is dead beside her. The danger of a wish that is insufficiently mediated upon is demonstrated in the case of the man, who is aware of his good-fortune at the present moment and wishes to remain forty-eight for the rest of his life. His life, therefore, ends almost immediately. But, as it happens, he has reached a stage when life is no longer necessary to him. The stranger has told him that desire stands behind everything and that it is essential to find out what one's desire is; but, on being asked what he himself would wish for, he admits that he can think of nothing:

> This reply astonished, almost alarmed me at first, but most curiously satisfied me on considering it.

The stranger also speaks of religion, life, death and mind—a host of things which 'were yet one single theme'. The product of Christianity finds himself faced with a religious man of the East, and while the atmosphere is intellectual, it is far more heady and exhilarating than the emotional religion to which he has been accustomed. The husband finds contentment at this point and so the desire to live is extinguished. The truth is that to desire is to be incomplete, Stephens believed; we may dream ourselves to seem whatever we want, but we will find that the only stable thing is He who creates us by his dream. We must discard our attachment to places or things, and fly swiftly to his truth. For we only reach nobility of soul when we can sing

> Empty am I
> Of everything,
> In every way.

The sense of being apart from other people comes into Stephens's work frequently, and not only people but objects and animals are separate too. As he wrote at the back of *Essays in Zen Buddhism*, perhaps in preparation for a poem:

> He is standing before the mountain
> He is *alone*, or he and the mountain
> Are alone, the sky spreads above them both
> And it is alone. There is a river
> Flowing down the slope. it is alone.

Other people do not really affect any essential part of us—it is what is in us that causes us the sensations of grief or anger. Our feeling that we have sinned comes from the guilt in our own minds and not from the accusation of others. We face our souls alone. But to lack responsibility and love and to feel separate from other creatures, Stephens considered, is vanity. It is to puff ourselves up with importance. This is what the character in 'Etched in Moonlight' experiences at the moment when he conceives hatred for the lovers. He feels a gulf of isolation dividing man from man. In reality we cannot be separate from other creatures unless we are separate from God, for we are all one in Him. But He is alone because He is the only thing that exists; and to be with Him is to be alone. We achieve this state by an effort of will. There all is lonely, all is beautiful and loneliness and beauty are everywhere. To be alone, in this exalted state, is Wisdom and Enlightenment.

Wisdom is the culmination of knowledge; and by knowledge we mean the revelation of God that is reached by erasing desire. Knowledge removes fear, which is the wisdom of ignorance, and there is no danger of it being used wrongfully by anyone, for it is only granted to those who are ready for it. Knowledge is the parent of love. It is higher than magic and its most advanced stage is equated with love itself. Love was a natural virtue to Stephens; he had always preached it and admired it in Blake. He believed that suspicion of our neighbour is the result of fear, and the evil we see in others, the projection of our own wickedness. Love is a spontaneous thing and can be received only by divine grace through the inspiration of knowledge. God and Beauty and Love are what the archangels talk about. There can be nothing greater; and Love is 'joy' and completion—it is very life to those who are ready for it.

> The mind that can hold joy must be strong indeed. I could no more contain it than I could round the sea in my palm; and almost as it had swirled into me, it swept out; leaving behind only that to which I had a right and which was my own,

laments the jealous man in 'Etched in Moonlight'. Joy is the Golden Bird who lightens all darkness and brings 'lovely life' to those who taste her freedom. In 'The Pit of Bliss', written in the early 'twenties, Stephens expressed his philosophy succinctly in a few phrases: Knowledge is insight, emotion is being, and Love is the essence and increase of these. Being, which is existence experienced to the full and union with the Self, is Joy. He noted the fundamental happiness in divine life in the back on Manilal N. Dvividi's *Imitation of Sankara*, writing:

He happy for this is to be
Bliss is the root of every tree
Or lacking this nothing can be.

In 'Theme with Variations', in *Kings and the Moon* (1938), Stephens examined the different ideas of love: love of life, love of people, and the conventional love in fairy tales; courtly love and love in marriage; but then he burst forth into a panegyric on the nature of real love, the all-embracing love of all creatures. Love and life are to be found in spontaneous existence, he declared, when one never notices what one is doing. This is, of course, equivalent to the highest philosophy in Buddhism, 'Work and be not concerned for the result,' and the rejuvenation of Spring and the discipline of one's mind contribute to realizing this achievement:

Spring-time
And the moon,
And love
—The three is ecstasy.

Love sees no distinction between the forms of being; Love feels equally for fly, spider, devil and God. Everything is beautiful to Love.

Do you love?
Then love are you
—No other knowledge shall avail—
To be, to know,
And so to do,
That is the truth, and all the tale.

Stephens's interest in Indian philosophy developed gradually and absorbed all the convictions he formed early in life with the exception of Blake's energy. This could not be included in a religion of subjectivity, as could Divine beauty, which Buddhists do not emphasize as strongly as Stephens did, and in which he continued to believe, perhaps on account of the intellectual support of Plotinus. But a sense of peace replaced the former 'lust of life', albeit a joyous, throbbing contentment entirely his own, and quite unlike the gravity of Buddhist peace. He never on the other hand discarded Christ's revelation as false, and indeed the tolerance of the Indians for other religions and ways to the divine was near to his heart. In an important poem in his

K

last book of verse he showed that subjective and objective religion complement each other and the ideas of their doctrines each give a part of the whole truth which we will perceive when the Divine is revealed. 'For the Lion of Judah', dedicated to Koteliansky, whom he nicknamed affectionately with Christ's Old Testament name, is based in form on 'The Phoenix and the Turtle', which has been ascribed to Shakespeare. He recalled a time of perfect love before the Phoenix, the symbol of rebirth and love, and the Dove, the symbol of peace and love, were parted. Mind and heart were complementary then. Now both are blind and treacherous and the Swan, the symbol of Beauty, sings the lament of mind and heart, reminding us that the intellect has governed Indian philosophy and the heart is dominant in Western religion. As he sings, he too must die. All hope, therefore, is gone from the world and men have no more 'the Dove, the Phoenix and the Swan' on whom to meditate. Stephens's Trinity of Christianity, Buddhism and Platonic abstract Beauty offer the alternative roads to salvation and are different aspects of the Divine; and in his late poetry he constantly linked what they stand for in his moods of exultation and praise:

> The Good, the Beautiful, the True,
> Is love,
> And loving
> And is you.

IX

Lectures in America and Return to London

The Red-Bud, the Kentucky Tree,
Bloomed the spring to life for me
In Freelands; and the Mocking Bird
—Nimble chorister of glee
Sweet as poet ever heard
In a world of ecstasy—
Sang the summer, and the sun;
Sang the summer in to me.
                    Christmas at Freelands

IN 1929 Stephen MacKenna, with whom Stephens enthusiastically discussed his esoteric beliefs, moved up to London to live
near his friend, first taking rooms in Kingsbury near 'Jamsey',
whence, perched on a bicycle, he sought more permanent lodg-
ing, and then in autumn 1929 settling into a little modern
house, 'Ellendene', at Harrow. Every Saturday night his guitar
playing friends would gather there among the books and the
Buddhas (Stephens often expressed his ambition to possess a
white porcelain Buddha); while during the week MacKenna
worked away at the final volume of his translation of Plotinus.
His life was frugal and he survived on the vegetable mess served
to him each evening by a woman who came in daily to help in
the house.

Theme and Variations, first published by itself in New York, and
then included, with additions, in *Strict Joy*—'Writ by James
Stephens for Stephen MacKenna on the 18th, 19th and 20th
January 1929, and typed by him a million times e'er it was
proper to send his friend on this 21st of January instant'—was
owed to MacKenna's translation of Plotinus, which had been
shown to Stephens at intervals as it slowly emanated. In Dublin

135

he had often heard A.E. and MacKenna arguing about Catholic and Indian mysticism, and he found much to agree with in Plotinus, whose central doctrine declared that virtue is knowledge. Wrong-doing, too, is not rebellion—Stephens still felt there was something cleansing in the struggle of good and evil —so much as bewilderment and weariness. Plotinus also stresses inner experience, the return upon oneself, and he speaks of the soul's desire for that One which alone can satisfy it. While his philosophy lacked the imaginative mysticism necessary for Stephens's temperament, the poet found, when he received MacKenna's translation, that it echoed many of his beliefs. He incorporated Plotinus's Ideal Beauty, a non-material principle, into his own version of Buddhism.

The subject of *Theme and Variations* is Beauty and its transience. We see the sunset at evening and are made thoughtful by the impermanence of its loveliness. The mind is ready to examine the meaning of all things and if our memory could only hold fast the beauty it experiences we would find wisdom waiting there for us. The *Variations* expand the Theme. God has created us and is in us. Our Desire and Mind have formed a dream world through their ignorance, but this is unsatisfactory as it is unreal, and causes us doubts. We are loath to renounce our doubts, however, as we fear that worse may enchain us. The irony is that God, living as He is within us, finds Himself trapped in the dream too. The universal Mind, which is courage, hope and loveliness, alone can illumine our blindness, arouse the slow, idle Will to pierce forgetfulness and annihilate Desire, the cause of ignorance. Our memory of true existence will then be restored. We have faculties of observation and preception, but they lie to us and the Mystery of Mysteries is hidden from them. However, God is behind all things and, with time, we will outgrow desire and dream. The almost perfect man wishes to leave them already. Stephens then foretells the annihilation of the world, but, in case this may horrify us too much, he reminds us that Nature is still full of life. This only causes more gloomy thoughts as we recall how animal preys on animal—it seems contrary to the law of love. We, also are part of the doomed sequence and death is ours too. However, we are comforted by the hope that perhaps, when Death comes, we may be tired and wish to sleep. Man, though bound up in his dreaming mood, is part of the divine All, and really creates doubt, misery and death in his own mind. These states do not exist but are part of the dream. No bird questions the safety of his wing; and the perfect man, too, dares to be alone and is tranquil:

> To be sufficient and alone
> Is Joy, and joy's rewarding kiss,
> Is ecstasy, and all of bliss
> That bird, or man, or god hath known.

These great men fly in 'the blank of Everywhere' and save themselves from the curse of evolution, which is the Mind, 'our angry ape'. All is transient but the Creator. The poet, who has the difficult task of singing about infinity, tells us of Spring, the symbol of eternal life in Nature; and it belongs to us. It alone, with the Self, is everliving.

This is the most coherent exposition of his beliefs until the final poetry, worked and reworked until Stephens was satisfied with its expression. Later he gathered such confidence in his views as to be monotonous in an extreme.

MacKenna's health deteriorated after his move to London —he had always been delicate—and he saw less and less of his friends in the few years before he died. James Stephens's movements must be traced elsewhere; and they are well documented in letters to Koteliansky, for Kot zealously preserved any communication from close friends. He began to write to him from America in 1929.

In April 1925 he had been to America for the first time on a lecture tour organized for him by Mary and Pádraic Colum, and before he went he speculated excitedly as to how he should dress. He had been in the habit of wearing an eye-glass to help his weaker eye, but John Brennan pointed out to him that this made him look like an Englishman, and he decided to refrain from using it during the tour. His first stop had been at Chicago, where he stayed with Mrs. Vaughan Moody, the widow of the poet, a Christian Scientist. She ran a business, 'Home Delicacies', which provided exotic food for parties. While staying with her Stephens contracted pneumonia, and he was very ill for a time, but he recovered under her excellent care. Then he went to W. T. H. Howe, later President of the American Book

Company, with whom he had been in correspondence for some years. Howe was interested in Stephens's manuscripts, for he wished to expand the Book Company's output to include other books than text-books, and he arranged for Stephens to come back to America later to help him to sort the books in his own private collection. The arrangement planned further lecture tours—or, rather, poetry recitals, interspersed with apposite comments and his own stories—on which Howe's agent would accompany him and offer the anthologies, to which Stephens had written introductions, for sale to the audiences; and Stephens enjoyed lecturing, and bore up well to the strain, as, according to MacKenna, he combined 'nerve placidity with intellectual agitation, a very enviable conjunction'.[1]

He wrote the foreword to Vasilii Vasilevich Rosanov's *Fallen Leaves, Bundle One*, which Kot had translated from the Russian, on the journey to America, and sent it to Kot for his opinion, from the S.S. *Leviathan*, on 12 August, 'at 6 hours sail from New York'.

> I had intended writing a different kind of introduction, But on
> the boat, my pen went off in another way, & this is the result . . .
> If your publisher doesnt care for it he need not print it.

The publisher must have approved because the volume was printed, in a limited edition, with the preface by Stephens, the same year.

Stephens spent some time in Mr. Howe's home studying his collection of books and writing essays; but he realized that he was being used for his popular appeal, and felt somewhat in the position of 'court jester', or entertainer, to Howe's friends and colleagues and was not at all happy in the association.

Back in London he would meet Kot on Wednesday evenings at the Monico Café in Piccadilly, or at Ridgeway's, and he had a practice of dashing off some of his poems for Kot's criticism:

> That
> (or the Thatness, or Suchness, or Thusness)
> That which is told of—That Thou Art,
> There is no other sprite
> No heaven, nor earth, nor middle part;
> There is no day or night;

[1] *Journal and Letters of Stephen MacKenna*, London, 1936, p. 215.

> There is no beauty, truth, nor wit,
> But That Alone
> And Thou Art it,

he scribbled on the back of an envelope, on 26 November 1930;
and a few years later, on a similar occasion, he wrote:

> I wish, my dear, but what I wish
> I dare not know, and cant explain:
> Who wishes hath not, and to wish
> Is to have lived in vain;
> I do not wish for anything:
> And shall not wish again.

The economy of this late style lent to too great facility of
expression and lack of content, and unfortunately his last poems
are all occupied with philosophical reasoning and incline to be
arid. *Theme and Variations* and *Strict Joy*, published in 1930 and
1931, which must be examined in connection with *Kings and
the Moon*, all display these traits and except that they are filled
with an intuitive understanding typical of Stephens, show no
other personal characteristic.

Sometimes the verses written at the Monico were frivolous,
as, for instance, on 2 September 1930:

> As I have a
> bad memory,
> I bought this
> for Kot,
> Hoping that he
> Me
> Has not forgot

or, when he had mistaken the date, he wrote:

> I had hoped to go to Ottoline & then write you of who was
> there & what we parleyed about, but, on Thursday, I thought
> it was Wednesday, & didn't find out the phases of the moon
> until the next morning.

> Altho' it was Thur,
> I thought it was Wed,
> There was such a blurr
> In my fool of a head:
> And I missed such a lot

Through my head being fat,
Having tea and a chat
With Philip and Ott.

In April 1932 he wrote to Kot on his way to Paris, saying,

I am sorry to miss even one of our meetings, for I think, as time goes on, that they get better & better.

But literary discussion continued in their letters, Stephens showing his whimsicality in his innate disgust at the prevalent erotic trend in literature:

22 May 1932

Dear Kot: Highbrow! You quote at, or toward me, from the Torah. It is good to be able to quote from one's own race, even, as it were, from one's own marrow: and to be not as the gentiles are, who, when they would quote, must subtly misquote: and must still depend for their wisdom on another effort than their own. You see, I am writing nearly as cryptically as you did. I have finished all that I shall read of the Dodge Lawrence book.[1] It is a fundamentally dishonest piece of work. Not dishonest by intention, but by temperament. What weak idiots are these vanity-ridden people! And by what shifts do they disguise weakness and semi-idiocy! And how they do seek, as in a frenzy, for values, where they so poignantly know no value is. Once people were hag-ridden: now even the hags are bed-ridden: and, with their tonsils out: their appendixes gone, their wombs removed, their bladders bust, and their guts in decay, they seek to woo & to be wooed! Only in bed is there hope, they say: only in bed is life. God help us all.

Forgive J. S.

He himself inclined to the romantic in matters of love, and to the formal in literature. He became a founder member of the Irish Academy of Letters in 1932, Yeats, Gogarty, A.E. and Montgomery Hyde were members too, and they planned a Book of the Irish Academy, to be published by Methuen, containing a contribution from each member. Stephens went to Dublin the following year to arouse interest in the venture and to collect material for the volume, but it came to nothing.

In early August 1932 he went to America again on the

[1] This must be one of D. H. Lawrence's books, but it is difficult to know which.

Cunard R.M.S. *Scythia*, and he asked Kot to keep him supplied with current English newspapers until he should return. 'Dear Kot,' he wrote:

> It is now the evening of the first day out. At 7 o'c. in the morning I'll see (if the Lord lets me get out of bed) Ireland. But I'm only writing this to beg something of you (me! who am always begging from you.) This is the beg. If at the end of each week you have any of the weekly papers 'Statesman' 'New English' please don't light your fire with them, but send them on to me in c/o W.T.H. Howe, 300 Pike Street, Cincinatti, Ohio, U.S.A. and so I'll be more or less up to date, & in touch, 'able to keep up with all ye wise ones when I go back, and, too, it will mitigate a certain loneliness. Míle agus grád mór agat.

Kot complied and continued to supply Stephens during his tour in America. He wrote in October, from Pike Street, to report on the progress of the anthology, which he published with E. L. Beck and R. H. Snow in 1933, as *English Romantic Poets*.[1]

> I am the busiest of men. I'm making a large-scale anthology, for my friend here, of the poetry of the 19th century. I never knew there was so much verse written until I began reading for this work. There are heaven knows how many thousands of writers in that epoch, and while some of them are responsible for about three thousand close pages, none, I think, fall below one thousand. They used to write in their sleep as well as in their wake. But I have been (and still am) enormously interested, and have been (and still am) working at the rate of at least eight hours a day. I have all the big ones done (and what big ones they were!) and the littler ones (most of whom are done also) are big enough for anyone today. By the way, and apropos des bottes—I read an article in *Hours in a Library*, or *Among my Books*, or some such title by Leslie Stephen Vol. 3. I've looked for, and found it *Hours in a Library*, it is. There is an article there on Coleridge which you should read in order to offset the article you got me to read in the Times Lit. Supp. by Murry. Taken by itself Murry's article is a piece of dreadful unfairness, and you should get to the antidote as quickly as may be. Coleridge was such and such and so, not a doubt of it, as also am I & you and

[1] His introduction was reprinted the following year in the other anthology they compiled, *Victorian and Later English Poets*, first published in New York in 1934.

Murry, but beyond all such suchnesses, and before the, and away from the, he was Coleridge—one who was respected and beloved by Lamb & Wordsworth, and by many another leal soul and wise. I miss enormously our meetings, and in especial, I miss Kot, The news you gave me about Sullivan[1] was not of the best. I brought his book here with me & a dozen people have read it with acclamation. I wrote, just a noteen of a note, to Ottoline a few days ago; and as I have nothing to write about (this letter being the proof) why I had nothing to tell her. Eight hours a day of 19th century poetry is, believe me, a grueller. Heigho, I'll get a book out of it and a penny, and live happy ever after!

He depended on Kot's interest as he travelled about, Kot was always helping his friends to the utmost; he was instrumental in providing Stephens with work on prefaces to new books. In his rather inconclusive preface to Dorothy Richardson's translation of Joseph Kastein's *Jews in Germany*, in 1934, Stephens celebrated friendship with a Jew, obviously becoming personal in this instance, after noting the debt of Christian culture to the Jewish world and applying his own term 'energy' to their contribution to contemporary arts:

> An imaginative Christian, or member of whatever other system, has but to enter into intellectual intimacy with a well-born Jew to realize that there are experiences within life of which he has no conception; that there are resolutions which he is never called upon to make: and resignations utterly unknown to the national life which shelters and encourages him, or the emotions which it permits and fosters: and that there are also courageous surmountings of difficulties and despairs, almost to be thought of as superhuman, and certainly to be considered as an honour to the race that could execute them.

He wrote from America again in 1934 about Dilys Powell's new book which was published on 4 October:

> You are an angel for sending me the papers: they have been a blessing. I didn't write because I have nothing to tell. Day follows day, & that's that. I got Dily's book: but there is nothing doing in the way you suggest. My friend would not

[1] J. W. N. Sullivan was one of their circle in London, a lovable music critic of unhappy temperament.

even look at it. Their shelves are packed with mss they can't print, &, because of the depression, they will never print. I do hope that the book has a success in London for the Cresset, & for her. I should like both the partners to be surprised and delighted. I see by the Observer that Miss Lewis is third impressioning. I hope Miss Dilys twentieths. I am reading it: have just finished the first essay—Lawrence—and she made one want to read the Lawrence poems, which I should have thought an impossible thing to make me want to do. Give her all my best hopes. I am going to lecture here & there about & will stay for a week at (N) Carolina University taking classes. My Byron is finished. Tis wonderful & beautiful, & strange, & marvellous.

Kot then sent him a collection of verse by Ruth Pitter, which the Cresset Press had just published, and Stephens liked it so much that he wrote a preface for the American edition, published by Macmillan in 1936. 'Are not you glad to publish so beautiful a thing,' he wrote on 17 October. In his preface he was to draw the distinction between great poets, minor poets, and bad poets, and pure poets of whom no criticism is possible. Ruth Pitter he placed in the final category with W. B. Yeats. In this letter he also spoke of Frieda Lawrence's autobiography, *Not I, but the wind*—'I find it not bad, tho' scrappy'. Frieda and D. H. Lawrence were part of the Kot clique, frequently at Lady Ottoline Morrell's house, with whom he had never become very intimate, largely because he disapproved so completely of Lawrence's work, and it is not unreasonable to suppose that disapproval was reciprocal, but, he conceded here, 'she does give a sense of herself & he'.

He returned to stay with W. T. H. Howe, in New York, while lecturing and he again spoke enthusiastically about Dilys Powell's book—'her book is actually the best thing that I have read by any of the immediate critics: and I do hope she gets some encouragement.' Lecturing, and moving about from place to place, where audiences fell for his charm and listened in wrapt admiration, but where he derived no stimulus from association with fellow intellects, tired him excessively. 'O Kot,' he wrote, 'get me a job, so that I don't have to do idiotic travellings!'

His spirits had risen in his next letter, from Durham, North

Carolina, on 15 November 1934, as he was looking forward to seeing his friends soon again:

> Thanks for the letters, & for all the news about Dilys, & Ruth Pitter, & Ottoline & Sullivan. I havent got the Lawrence book. Only read it in Kentucky. I am non-news of any kind. But that my spirit perks a bit at the thought that my Odyssey here is nearly over, & that I'll see you again. Just before Christmas expect to have a drink with me.

But it was a temporary return, because lecturing was the only method by which he could earn money now; the prefaces, the only writing he was doing, brought in very little. In August 1935 he missed Kot before catching the boat, and wrote a swift note of farewell:

> Over there when I'm doing nothing I've nothing to write about, & when I'm doing something I'm too busy to write: but you write to me a little oftener than you can.

That October he was interviewed by Cyrus F. Rice of the *Milwaukee Journal* at Madison, Wisconsin, about eighty miles from Milwaukee. The account of the interview appeared on the editorial page with a two column caricature of Stephens by Fred Sample. Stephens had been to read some of his poetry at the University of Wisconsin's Memorial Union Theatre. He was suffering from the effects of ptomaine poisoning which he contracted in Chicago from a dish of shrimp. His manager, a man from Macmillan's, was even sicker than Stephens was and remained in bed; but Stephens by great effort made the journey of one hundred and sixty miles to Madison, accompanied by a substitute manager. There he was rewarded by a packed house of students who had come to hear him and his charm, as everywhere in the United States, won the instant attention of his audience, and in spite of his fatigue and illness he succeeded in mesmerising them. Mr. Rice has said that Stephens's tiny stature and sad face were the things that first impressed him.

The interview took place in the bar where Stephens chose a martini, saying 'it lasts you longer than any'. He drank only one glass. 'This is my first today,' he said. 'You know, I love liquor. I really do. When I was younger I loved women and

God, but now I love liquor and God. That is pure love.' He continued in this flippant manner, discoursing on Joyce, Dublin, O'Casey and Stephen MacKenna, and he also referred to Gogarty. 'Joyce made him out a terrific snob. Of course he is, but a brilliant mind.'

While he tired desperately of the sentimental adoration, he enjoyed playing his role before the American audience and the English, and the travelling brought him into contact with sights he would otherwise have missed. He later used to tell a story about one of his lectures in America. He said that he was sitting on the platform in the lecture hall, trembling while the Chairman made the speech of introduction. He felt that every one else was towering over him, and he dreaded the moment when he would be called upon to rise and speak. Suddenly he noticed a dog coming down the gang-way between the rows of people, trotting steadily until it reached the platform, when it climbed up and came over to him. So encouraged was he by this support that he set to his lecture on English literature without any further qualms, and made it one of the best that he had ever delivered.

He loved coloured people; and another story he told of his time in America was full of gratitude to a negro. He slipped on the platform of a street car and lost his balance. An arm instantly shot out and scooped him back on to the street car just in time, and he found himself looking up in to a coal black face. Stephens said that he had never seen such love and tenderness on a stranger's face before.

There is no doubt that Stephens owed a great deal to his tours in America. Apart from the ensuing fame and popularity, he developed a style of speaking that was strictly individual and which stood him in good stead when he came to broadcast. He earned large fees and these proved useful in later years. His other patron, besides W. T. H. Howe, was Cornelius Sullivan of Wall Street, who took Stephens in hand, 'invested' his residue, and sent him back happy and prosperous. In December 1935, Stephens wrote to Kot from New York, nostalgically, to say that he would soon be back:

> It is bitterly cold up here, and will be 40 below zero in Maine when I get there. Moving about this way I am now (17,000 miles in six weeks) there is nothing to write about; just places,

& they are all the same place, & people who are always the same people, and lectures by me, which are always the same lectures; and trains, & trains, & trains, & now snow, & snow, & snow.

On 16 December he was on the way home for the last time on board the *Aquitania*, and on Christmas Day Kot joined him and Mrs. Stephens for dinner.

Stephens's next piece of work was his preface to Ruth Pitter's book of verse, *A Trophy in Arms*, which was published in New York in 1936. It was written and rewritten, as everything was now, and the final version was sent to Kot from Paris in June 1936:

> Will you handle the proof, & not send it any more to me, for I could go on writing it until Tib's Eve & the morning of the pealing of the last trump,

he said in despair. He had been seeing Joyce and his wife, but was soon back in London again and meeting Kot on Wednesday evenings once more.

Kot was very unwell later in 1936, and Stephens visited him and wrote to him to keep him in touch with what his friends were doing:

> It is a relief to all your friends that you have decided to rest & be attended. I think you will find that two weeks of being cared for will be better than two months of taking no care of yourself. I note you say the people there dont welcome visitors yet. One day, soon, send me a card again to tell me how you are shaping, & that I may call for quarter of an hour. Me, I have no news: except that the summer is soon to come, according to the papers, & that I am still hoping that Spain will whip her rebels, & that the Daily Mail is a pig. Will you, do you think ever need books or magazines, or whatnots of whatever description. In all the sort of things I am yours to command: so dont neglect to command, advise and howl to
>
> Your affectionate
James Stephens.

In September, after many of the usual delays, he returned with his wife to Paris for a couple of weeks, and wrote to Kot from his flat in Rue Campagne Première:

Here is merely a note, to say, first, that I have nothing to say, & to say, second, that when one has nothing to say, or to do, one can still have something to hope: therefore, I hope you are 99¾% better than you were two weeks ago. We may be here for another week: so, if you find time—no: dont write, for we may be back within the week, and I'll then give you a ring. From this part of the world there is no news. The newspapers are, even designedly, dull: they tell, in a lower tone, all that the Daily Mail, et all, squawks. But this city is unhappy, & is waiting for the problematicalist morrow. Personally, I think, in every despite, that the world-weather is 'set fair', & that if we can merely weather the next two years we shall have weathered a whole lot of weather. Of my own self I have nothing to say, A sense of 'interim' is so pronounced within me, and without, that almost I dont exist, or am merely a semi-suspended animation. Three nights ago we dined with Joyce at the other (the wrong) side of the city. There is a man who is almost happy. He bothers, that is, if he bothers at all, about his own botherations, and, in so far as I can see it, he doesn't bother one smallest part of a demi-damn about the world and its waggings. But he is nice— which, perhaps, is no great virtue, but is assuredly nowhat whatever of a vice. We argued, & quarreled, and made up on a Reissling wine, all about Ibsen—Joyce and Kot are of an equal weakness there, for Kot and Joyce do both applaud that one who is deplored by this one. Next day Joyce left in at my taudis[1] an Ibsen book *Little Eyolf &c*, & I have just replied to him that, on the strength of this alone (buttressed by all his other works) Ibsen is the only example of the literary sadist that western literature has known. As you see, I am writing you about nothing, having nothing to write about. Joyces opinion, & mine, & yours, about Ibsen! If that isnt the very inner non-being, & non-guts of nothing believe me mistaken even in science & mathematics, which twain, knowing nothing of I can't be mistaken in. My Hebrew also cannot be attacked, but my Irish is bad.

In October Kot had recovered, so the usual arrangement of meeting at Pagani's at 7 o'clock on Wednesdays resumed. Only when one of them was away, and Stephens was frequently in Paris, was the arrangement upset. On 11 January 1937, Stephens wrote to Kot when he returned from Paris to London:

---

[1] Slang in French for 'wretched hole'. Literally 'dog-hole'.

Here am I back again. Got in last night. I looked through all the book shops in Paris for something to send you, but could not find a thing. Can we meet on Wednesday. If not give me a ring. If you dont ring then seven o'clock as usual.

However in the coming months difficulties arose, other engagements and illness, and on one occasion the meeting had to be cancelled because the heavy traffic on the day of the Coronation daunted both writers. The friendship continued on paper, and Stephens often sent Kot his views on current publications, or snatches of what he himself was writing—

> Here is my newest poem, just made.[1]
>
> Nigh a river swollen by spring,
> Watching growth of everything
> And what joy the moon can bring.
>
> Thinking love is of the moon,
> And that love is over soon,
> And that love is all his boon.
>
> Thinking he had better pray
> To God, or woman, as he may,
> Or to the moon, that slips away.

In June 1937 he wrote to Kot about May Sarton's book of verse, *Encounter in April*:

> I'm sending back Miss Sarton's book. I ran right through it in one reading. It is all good &, at times, more than that. In especial I liked *On the Atlantic. The Trees. Evening Landscape. Portrait of the Artist. Portraits of three women. Slight Death. Song for Drought*, which I liked better than anything else. *To the Weary* also is lovely. So for *Keats & Mozart*. The first sonnet in especial, but all the sonnets. I expect on further reading I might like others more, but for an impression there is my just & mere impression. Tis a good book by a good writer.

He had met Miss Sarton through the Huxleys, whom he used to visit at their flat in Whipsnade or at the Administration Building in Regent's Park Zoo. Of all the animals that clustered about their rooms he must most have delighted in the bush baby which would leap from the top of the curtains to a visitor's shoulder and join the guests at the dinner-table to sip chocolate mousse delicately.

[1] Dated 20 June 1937.

X

Later Poetry

'Why do you live on the bank of a river?' . . .
    'Because a poem is a revelation, and it is by the brink of run-
ning water that poetry is revealed to the mind.'
    'How long have you been here?'
    'Seven years,' the poet answered.
    'It is a long time,' said wondering Fionn.
    'I would wait twice as long for a poem,' said the inverterate
bard.

Irish Fairy Tales

ON the morning of Christmas Eve, 1937, Stephens received a
severe blow. James Naoise, his only son, was killed in an
accident. He was deeply affected by the death of his son. He
never referred to him again during his lifetime but he withdrew
into himself even more, and cut a part of himself off completely
from his family and friends. He had almost ceased to write
poetry, and now, except for the sentence or two jotted down in
the books he was reading, abandoned verse altogether.

In company he was the same old James, and was still as
loquacious as he had been. He delighted Ruth Pitter and
Kathleen O'Hara when he visited them for dinner at their home
in Chelsea in June 1938.

'Ten years ago,' wrote Miss K. O'Hara in her journal in
1938, 'before we knew him, I heard him broadcasting, and I
wrote to Ruth that "his voice was like rain falling on velvet".'

(*Dark* velvet, R.P. adds). I little thought we should ever know
him so well. Like a good many Irishmen, he had caressing ways,
and calls one Sweetheart or Sweetest. He is so small, and had
such a large well-shaped head, piercing brown eyes; very poor
physique. At dinner he gave most of his food to Purser, our 24 lb
cat, with whom he was simply delighted, continually talking to
him and admiring his 'cunning' ways. Said he 'I would like to

149

L

have one of his kittens', but I told him, 'alas, he would never have any.' The first time he and Purser met, the latter stood in front of him, looked hard, then gave a prodigious yawn. 'What a Cauldron'! said J.S.

Stephens also related, in his Stephens manner, the description of the ceremony where he received the Polignac Prize:

'If it's money we're to get,' he said to his wife, 'we'd better get well to the front, so that we can—ah—get it.' Once the cheque was in their hands, they raced off to the station and so to Paris, where they had a little flat, to have a good time while it lasted, quite innocent of the fact that a banquet had been prepared, at which they were to have been, of course, the guests of honour.

In 1938 he published his last book of verse, *Kings and the Moon*, a collection of what he had been writing during the thirties. His final style, as we have seen, was utterly impersonal, and so the reverse of what had been so typical of his most productive period, and again his work is indicative of that strange link with Yeats whose later technique he greatly admired.[1] There was no development in method from that in *Theme and Variations* and *Strict Joy*. He was using the poetry of these books as a medium for his religious ideas and even his impish sense of fun had disappeared. The metres vary according to mood: eight-syllabled lines are common, groups of three objects, and verses in triplets are frequent too; but all metres have their roots in the conversational approach characteristic of his best verse. While at first sight his metres appear irregular, when read aloud many are found to be in strict form; for he continued to place words which required emphasis at the end of each line, regardless of the visual effect on the completed verse. For instance, in 'Gathering the Waters', he broke up the second couplet, to emphasize the word 'seeking':

> I have wasted
> Precious time!
> —Seeking
> What is nowhere found—.

The basing of his metres on the spoken word also meant that his verses were nearly always syllabic. It is certain that to

[1] Preface to *A Trophy in Arms*.

Stephens himself the metres were more regular than they appear to be on paper, because he heard them in his mind, and the pauses had as much importance in his verse forms as rests have in music. Phrase is balanced against phrase, the rhymes enriching the sound of the whole, but not determining the form of the poem. For instance, in 'Bidding the Moon', the first two verses when taken together are seen to make up four couplets, each of eight syllables. The second verse is not written in its couplets, however, for 'heart' requires emphasis:

> In blue, anew,
> The heart
> Takes thought,
> And thought is told in every part.

Similarly, in the second half, the verses are based on phrases of six syllables, varied in one place, with phrases of four syllables. The second part of 'Royally' in 'Kings and Tanists' consists of three-lined verses; yet, when examined closely, the metre is found to be in four couplets of eight syllables each.

Regular metres were written still, as in 'Sarasvati', though even blank verse was sometimes subject to the arbitrary stress of single words; but this, in 'Trumpets in Woodland', gave a fine result, every possible sound being wrung out of the bare words, and the phrases contributing music to the whole. He continued to experiment with technique. Part XXI of *Theme and Variations* has verses of eight-syllabled lines rhyming in couplets or triplets, but the first verse consists of two lines, the second is a triplet, and so on up till the last verse which has seven lines and holds the climax.

In general, however, the system in these final poems is different. The effort was towards a greater unity of thought in each single poem. This was achieved partly through inter-phrasing between verses. Rhymes usually couple themselves in pairs of verses, and common rhyme among the last lines of verses is frequent. Rhyme is used very much at whim, occasionally to give the effect of increased emotion, as in the very beautiful love-poem 'The White Swan', where the alternate rhymes of the first verse are broken in the second as the climax builds up:

Could you but see her
—She would seem
Like some bright star
That is seen in dream:
Like a sun-burst
Seen on a wintry day
When all, but one bright spot,
Is grey.

Could you but see her
—That would be
As when one sees
On a flooding sea
The white foam ride;
Or sees a proud swan,
Buoyantly,
Breasting a tide.

A common device was the breaking up of a regular metre when the meaning of the poem became more apparent, or when the poet's personal feelings could no longer be contained. In 'Envying Tobias', the first part states the dryness of modern religion: the second then discards the confines of the short lines in a desperate prayer for a guardian angel. 'Student Taper' is similar, consisting of two verses with the set phrases of a prayer divided from each other by a genuine plea in the suppliant's own words. The regular form of 'Gathering the Waters' is used to state how the poet originally sought satisfaction in a religion of reason; but this breaks up when he reaches to the Moon, the true Goddess, in adoration, praying to her for help and 'quickening' power. Then he turns to a chanting rhyme which mocks the power of the Moon. It is jerky, though in regular form, and only attains smoothness of tone when it tells the truth:

All is pure, and all is lovely:
All is so, and doth endure.

There is another use of the varied metre in 'Bidding the Moon'. The beginning of the poem is incantatory and traditional. Heraldic colours are used to symbolize the different kinds of joy, and, the poem indicates, after being brought to enlightenment through them, one may see into the deeper meanings of life. At this point the metre becomes richer, and the phrases more greatly sustained. In 'Royally', however, where the injunction is given in the first part and the result in the second, there is no change in metre because nothing personal has been touched. Shorter lines interspersed in metres which are predominantly long indicates a pause for thought, as in *Theme and Variations*, Part II; and in 'The Outcast', written in 1930, the shortened metre of the second conveys a feeling of depression and nothingness.

The metres which consist of short lines only, in these late esoteric books, work from a conclusion, either mocking an idea, or stating a principle for a disciple. Long-lined poems, on the other hand, are devoted to the study of some problem and use the verse-form to resolve it. Language is intentionally purer, offering ideas in the fewest possible words; but archaisms are still frequent, and still characteristic of Stephens's verse—'an you let it', 'saith' and 'searcheth'. As a contrast he was not afraid to use slang in titles—that of 'In the Red' saves the poem from being utterly depressing—or in phrases; and in some places his concision is dramatic. *Theme and Variations* tells how, without a chance to protest, we are all hurled into the void

> Where life saith—No I go not—and is gone!

He did not use the refrain technically, as Yeats used it. With Stephens it was a poetic device for description or for giving force to some idea. It began simply as the repetition of a phrase in the early poems:

> She had not got a place to fall
> And rest herself—no place at all.

This developed and repetition was used in the first line of a verse to give continuity from the previous verse. In 'The Snare' and 'The Centaurs', where it is done throughout the poem, there is an effect of crescendo to a climax. 'The Rivals' draws further music from the refrain:

> I didn't listen to him
> For he didn't sing to me.

But in his later verse he realized how useful a refrain could be to the meaning of a poem. Verses often share a common last line. The alteration of a refrain is dramatic:

When I was young
I had no sense
—Now I'm older
None have I:

But, over the hills,
And far away!
—Now I'm older
There am I.

In 'Gathering the Waters' the refrain resembles a dialogue very much in the manner of Psalm 24. In 'Theme with Variations' the recurring couplet in one section of the poem contains the pitch of the poem and the interpolations are embroideries on the main soaring theme:

No pride hath he who sings of escape from love:
All songs of escape from love are songs of despair;
Who so hath gat him away hath got nowhere.

Titles were important to him; he was always altering them and looking for suitable ones which would give a clue to the content of a poem. In 'Lullaby with Drums' the word 'Lullaby' emphasizes the sleeping, dead element of the sterile heart, and drums beat and beat remorselessly with the pessimistic theme; and the title 'Wild Dove in Wood-Wild', together with the first line of the last verse, echo the song of the dove and create a mood of tenderness in this beautiful love-song. Titles have another aspect of interest also. In the change of 'The Tinker's Brat' to 'Soft Winds' in *Collected Poems* a mellower Stephens gave the love of the mother the central position in the poem. 'The Nodding Stars' became 'The Devil'; he was more conscious of literary finesse. When he was young and an ardent revolutionary his poems were full of fantastic ideas, but looking back he realized that this one was unconventional and the ideal must be attributed to the Devil. The lack of awe in 'The Proud Mountains' appeared more outrageous when he changed the title to 'The Paps of Dana', since Dana is the mother of the gods (in Celtic mythology), and so the level of fantasy was raised beyond the point at which it was reality to him. His belief that music and poetry are inextricably linked is manifest in the names 'Cadence', 'Arpeggio', 'Theme with Variations', and 'Minuette'; and the headings 'Nora Criona' and 'The Girl I left Behind Me', taken from Irish songs, play a part in the music of the verses themselves.

Stephens had become thoroughly self-conscious in his later work; his expression had altered radically and though there is much of excellence, there is much typical of his early style to be desired:

> His beard swung on a wind far out of sight
> Behind the world's curve;

or the description of hair:

> Straight as a stream balanced upon the wind,

could never be found in the later verse. Before it had always been a relief to get back from the flights of imagination and horror to 'the broad-backed Earth' with its comforting solidity. Nature at that time was regarded from the reality of the human world, leaf,

> With thin pointed claws
> And a dry dusty skin,

and wind being personified; but this more or less died out. The former vigour of attack was a sad loss. Yet the vigour was only dormant, toned down in an attempt at conventional literary style. The same Stephens was there whole-heartedly. In the first books effects had been achieved through descriptions rather than by technique, and he still rejected artificial devices sternly and sought results through sheer force of personality. In 'The Sinner', in 1912, the imploring man entreated a hearing from God, holding the closing clouds back with 'a clutching hand'; and it was natural that, when Stephens's poetic ideas confined themselves to esoteric doctrine, it was the power of his beliefs that carried the verse along. Figures of speech are rarely found. Symbols were limited to the commonplace. In 'The Voice of God' grass, tree, mountain and man represent life; the figure of King Billy in 'College Green' is a sufficient reminder of English domination,[1] while Deirdre (even, it is of interest to

---

[1] This statue stood in College Green in Dublin for 150 years and was a target for insurgents before finally it was removed. Yeats uses it in 'Lapis Lazuli', *Collected Poems*, London, 1955, p. 338.

notice, in the novel) is not the heroine of a lost heroic myth, but is the archetype of all beautiful women. Religious imagery was taken directly from the Bible. In 'Envying Tobias', the well-known story gives point to the poem, and in 'I Am' Stephens was able to telescope the immensity of God into a brief phrase. He twice used Plato's cave in *Songs From the Clay*, a time when he was interested in him. The road in another poem symbolized progression. Yeat's 'mask' appears once, in *Theme and Variations* XX; but, in general, Stephens's symbols are even simpler than these. He created images with everyday objects, such as sour milk, withered weeds, apples, buds, honeycombs; and the bird, symbolic to all minds of freedom, which became 'The Golden Bird' in *A Poetry Recital*, always sings of 'joy'. Reason is 'like a tin-can in the sun'. In *Theme and Variations* XXI dogs embody the idea of the lowness of man, who seeks heavenly things, yet is doomed to return to the earth. The choice of skunk, badger and sow as animals to be worshipped, in 'To Lar with a Biscuit', shows that Stephens felt ideals in the modern world had become degraded.

Conventional symbols, however, derived special strength from the mode of their presentation, for they were always drawn from personal experience and so described. For instance, convention tells that the moon rises when night falls. In reality it is in the sky for hours before that and James Stephens, in 'Student Taper', lights his lamp 'at the mid of moon'. Similarly, 'the mid and grim of night' gives a clear picture of a frightening hour.

The most important single symbol to be found in Stephens's work is the Moon. It is not accorded undue prominence in the earliest of his writings, though choosing the name 'Cynthia' for his wife indicates that the moon already had some special significance for him. In *The Hill of Vision* its attraction is obvious; Eve describes herself as

> the moon upon a night
> All alluring.

He also referred to 'moon-peace'; but he first turned to the moon as a religious symbol in *Songs From the Clay*, where it is the moon who announces to the world that 'there is no sin'. In 'The Rune' and in 'A Song for Lovers' he noted the link of the moon with the sea—'they love each other well'. This developed a controlling image for his last veise. There 'the lonely soul swings lonely in the sea' but the moon, who gathered scattered waters to a point, is the answer to the lonely soul's longing. The moon is remote. She is passive, where the fiery sun is not, and so a suitable symbol for Indian mysticism. (The sun could be used as an image for Christianity, though Stephens did not in fact so employ it.) Moon-religion is esoteric and requires personal discipleship and devotion, for, as Stephens says in 'Theme with Variations', she is liable to slip away. The moon shines in the night of man's ignorance. Her light for Stephens represented the means for reaching the ideal state; and the symbol of the moon gave full force to the exposition of his doctrine for life in his poetry:

Light floods the mind!
And now the mind is pure,
Is naught-intent,
Is empty:

It is withdrawn into its solitude,
—As the moon withdraws,
When storm and rain have blacked the world away,
And only the great gold sun rides on the main—

The Shining Ones are vanished
In greater splendour,
Withdrawn, not lost, in gold,
The light not gone away:

Stars and the moon
Are lost in the light of life,
As the pure mind, withdrawn,
Is lost in the light of God.

XI

Broadcasting

I knew an old man in Connaught one time, and he was a great lad for the stories. He used to make his money at it, and if that man was to break off in the middle of a tale the people would stand up and kill him, they would so. He was a gifted man, for he would tell you a story about nothing at all, and you'd listen to him with your mouth open and you afraid that he would come to the end of it soon, and maybe it would be nothing more than the tale of how a white hen laid a brown egg. He would tell you a thing you knew all your life and you would think it was a new thing. There was no age in that man's mind, and that's the secret of storytelling.

The Demi-Gods

THE War affected Stephens and Koteliansky, as everyone about them, very deeply. The feeling that the world was breaking up had begun with the abdication of Edward VIII. Stephens's friends and benefactors were all in sympathy with the Establishment, and from them he adopted a Tory attitude, lamenting Edward VIII's decision in 'The Flowers of the Forest'. As soon as war was declared he abandoned his inborn pacificism, now completely pro-British, and in 1940 he wrote to *The Times* declaring that he wished to elect himself an Englishman for as long as the situation remained as it was, thus deprecating Irish neutrality which Kot had denounced severely to all he encountered. His outer life was not disrupted at first, though it is said that he helped the Ministry of Information in Malet Street, dealing with Irish affairs and doing some translation, and he continued to visit Paris as he had done in the First World War. He was there in February 1939, after visiting Birmingham to broadcast on Yeats, and he went back for a week in February 1940. However, his next move was to evacuate to Gloucestershire.

Woodside was a small cottage near a village called Sapperton, about six miles from Cirencester. It was an ordinary four-roomed cottage built on to a disused chapel. The chapel was about the same size as the cottage—it had held a congregation of about fifty people—but it was not divided into rooms. At that time neither building had modern conveniences of any kind, and the only water supply was a well by the front door. Woodside had been rented by Angus Morrison and his wife and it was their habit to spend their Easter and summer holidays there. In September 1939 Mrs. Morrison remained after her husband had gone home, but the conditions in winter with two small children to look after were too primitive and the following January she returned to London; later the Morrison family moved to Cambridge. When the Blitz started the Rothensteins, who were living across the valley from Woodside, at Far Oak, approached Mr. and Mrs. Morrison to let the empty cottage to the Stephenses who wanted to be away from London and the raids. The Stephenses stayed in the cottage for some months before taking over the lease from the Morrisons in May 1941; they then made their own improvements, and lived there until the war ended and though the isolation depressed Stephens, he was delighted at leaving the city.

The surrounding countryside was enchanting and quite unspoiled, and there were steep hills on either side of the valley. There was one other cottage quite near by, and a glimpse of cottages down the lane where the post box was; but Woodside was completely isolated. It was not on the road. It was approached by a path which ran along the side of a sloping beechwood; on the other side of the minute cottage garden there were open fields and a view across to Far Oakridge where the Rothensteins' house was situated. One of the improvements made by James and his wife was to divide the chapel up into rooms, so that Stephens would have somewhere to work, and they fitted in a kitchen range to warm the place and lighted it with paraffin lamps. Mrs. Stephens applied her gifts for house-keeping and the dwelling became cosy and comfortable, and she worked at the small garden with great success.

They lived an isolated life, with visits to Stroud or Cirencester about once a week for shopping, and then Stephens had an opportunity to browse about book shops or to look at antiques.

Mrs. Stephens also took the car to the train to collect him on his return from London from broadcasting. It is said that Stephens cut himself off and lived largely in the chapel, and it is certainly true that he found the period in Gloucestershire rather depressing though characteristically he derived great enjoyment from working the pump. His first letter to Kot was written in October 1940 when they had just settled in and before they had arranged about the lease.

> Dear Kot, Apologies to you for not having written, but I am about six miles from a town, and the getting of a bottle of ink was a whole job. I am living in a disused Chapel, which has nothing whatever in it, except a fire-place, & we live like the people of the primitive and the prime. One goes out every day to draw water, and to pick up sticks for the fireplace, but I dont doubt but that we shall be the chilliest people of earth when the winter comes. Already this place, it is on the topmost reach of the Cotswolds, it is as cold as winter does be in London, & will be colder. I was in town about ten days ago, went up with Rothenstein, got there at 12.30, rehearsed at the B.B.C. till one, had lunch, returned B.B.C. at 2, spoke at 2.30 had to meet R'stein at 3, & catch, with him, the 4.30 for Stroud, & drive back here. So I was unable to see you, or even try to. I'm going up again shortly to speak, but dont know when; and doubt that I'll be able to get in touch with you during the, perhaps, half hour that I'll have free. Bombs fall here every night, same as elsewhere, for we have aerodromes around & about, & it seems that we protect the Port of Bristol. I havent seen one newspaper since I left London, but we've a small portable wireless thing which gives the exact same news every time we turn it on. All love to you, my dear, send me an occasional letter.

Kot did write (it is a great pity that his letters have not survived), and he kept Stephens constantly supplied with cigarettes, for he was a very heavy smoker.

> 15 Dec 1940
> Dear Kot. The postman came this morning with your parcel. What a mighty lot of cigarettes! I smoked ten of them—one after the other, and—as God looking on the world thought it good —the only silly thought He ever had—so, smoking them, I knew them good. Cigarettes get more & more difficult to get, even Woodbines; so you may guess how astonished I was to get your hundred thousand. I'll try to make them last a long time. A very

nice chap, named Angus Morrison, owns this chapel. He is a musician, plays a lot on B.B.C. programmes (piano). He & his lady called in the other night to see us (from Bristol). Do you know him at all? I havent seen a Sunday paper, or a weekly, since I left London. The only daily is the Daily Mail, & it doesnt always get here. I'll be glad to Sunday-Times-write if they want me to. Morrison told me that the B.B.C. has been badly bombed again. There are always bombs about these parts, but the parts are so wide, and hilly and valley that one doesn't mind them. I wish we were back in London. I wish we had never left it. I wish I was getting the everynight bombing that London, and you, is getting. I wish I could see you every Wednesday. I wish I could see you every day of the week. I wish that U and I, and D[1], and whatever alphabeticals you would elect for, could be meeting together once a week, and lunching together once a day, and dining together every night; and that, thereon, we all went to bed together. How delicious t'would be, then, for us all to breakfast together: and, thereon, to start getting ready for lunch, and dine, and bed and board with ourselves, and with none others whatever. As far as the world is concerned I am indifferent—but, I like my loves! From these parts there is no news, nor ever will be—There is nothing whatever here except Cotswolds, and the almost nightly bombing of them. But there are, imperceptably (I saw them) squirrels in the trees, looking for nuts that don't exist; and foxes in the hinterlands looking for hens that are triply wired in. God blast the Allemands; but God help the squirrels, and the foxes, and the strayed cats, & the good, brave, diligent, hungry, masterless dogs—And the crows that look for something where nothing is, and U, and I, and D, who have only got a bit, where we, perhaps, hoped for a piece. I have just finished, and sent off to him (you dont know him) a preface, or prefatory writing, to his new book.[2] If the book ever comes out I'll direct him to send it to you. Other than that I am merely a lost soul, wishing to die, or to be back in London. Give my love to our loves! But what is that? Philosophically, and annually, I begin to be querulous about wisdom and love, and to be interested only in who so I like; and in the craft of verse.

One of his friends in the B.B.C. was John Grenfell Williams, who was Head of the Colonial Service. Stephens used to meet

[1] Dilys Powell.
[2] E. R. Eddison: *A Fish Dinner in Memison*, New York, 1941.

him and the Pacific Service Director, Robert McCall, from time to time for a meal, a tiny figure under his deerstalker hat. On the first of these meetings, at lunch in a little restaurant in Soho, after he had dabbled with his food for a short time, Stephens produced from his pocket a Manilla envelope and he proceeded to shift the balance of his plate into it. When his friends asked him what he was doing he told them that he had made friends with a little dog which he had encountered near his home and which seemed to be hungry, and that whenever possible he took it something to eat.

Broadcasting gave him a new lease of life. Joseph MacLeod, the well-known newsreader once told how he nearly lost his job at the B.B.C. through James Stephens. Stephens was sitting on a long stool, his legs curled up under him like a leprechaun, reading a short story at the microphone before the news was due to begin. He had reduced everyone in the studio, including MacLeod remarked, the Scots engineers, to tears at the pathos of his tale, through the pitiful tone of his voice as he related it. MacLeod became so choked up that he could not read the news until five minutes after the scheduled time, and this at one of the more critical moments of the War. Stephens, on the other hand, hopped off the stool merrily and went out to drink with his friends. He was in his element, for he had always been famed for his monologues, and he put as much work into his broadcasting as he had put into his writing, embroidering freely on any material that came to hand. When reading 'A Glass of Beer' he related his idea of the circumstances in which the original Irish poem had been written, facts which have no scholarly foundation at all; but he was completely at home in the oral tradition of his country and allowed himself full license in the medium of storytelling. In *Irish Fairy Tales*, his first opportunity for practice in this genre, he described the King of Leinster's cows with affection as if he had seen them himself: 'There was nobody in the world could have avoided loving those cows: such cows they were! such wonders!'; and in other places, too, he entered into the tale himself in spirit. The attractiveness of his prose style was due to his ability as a conversationalist, and his stories in *Irish Fairy Tales* were commenced in the traditional manner, mentioning some point of interest which would catch the attention of the listener: 'We do not know where Becfola came from. Nor do we know for certain where she went to,' and so on.

These qualities of personality assured his appeal as a broadcaster, for he was completely at ease in front of the microphone. He prepared his manuscripts with most careful attention and mastered a distinctive method of attacking the material before him. He would begin with some definite or controversial statement, such as 'William Blake is an oddity', or perhaps refer to something utterly obscure, in order to arouse the curiosity of his audience. Then he developed his theme; but still he had the elusiveness of a bird, darting away from the subject, and returning to it at an oblique angle:

> Some years afterwards I became very interested in words. I just adored a certain dictionary that said 'Wine, weal and winegar are werry good wittles I wow', but I began to notice that there are certain things, quite a number of them, and we have no words really to describe them at all. 'Tis so with water. We have lots of dry words, for we are dry creatures, but at the best our wet words are only damp, and so we don't ever get intellectually or imaginatively at that element at all. All that is just a prelude to the fact that I want to tell you about the happiest male creature that I have ever known or heard of.

He seized any opportunity of enlarging upon some relatively minor point with delight.

Poetry, as we have seen, had always been for Stephens not a written but an oral art. As early as 1907 he wrote, 'True Poetry is the union of Wisdom with Melody; neither of which are complex at their best, but are based on a big broad simplicity.'[1] He broadcast and staged readings of his own verse regularly and he worked at each performance with all his art. Each word was pronounced very definitely, and he was accustomed to sway while he was reading, thus emphasizing the rhythm, and to act every idea contained in the poem at the same time—the vanity of the mountains in 'The Paps of Dana', and so on. He obviously enjoyed every minute of the recitals. In his broadcasts he was completely natural and happy in front of the microphone, telling stories of Dublin circles, and occasionally breaking into song. David Marcus met him in a Lyons restaurant

[1] 'Poetry' (*Sinn Féin*).

once, shortly before his death, and described how Stephens was able to attract the attention of every one else in the room:

> I was completely gripped as I watched the rubbery face before me reflect every intonation and mood; the eyes would open wide apart and then slumberingly peer through almost closed lashes, and then be swallowed entirely by the bosomy lids that enveloped them. The hands would draw the poem all about me in the air and the massive-seeming head would sway and float like a barrage-balloon in a breezy day.[1]

Everyone near by began to listen, and Stephens broke incorrigibly into 'the only poem in the English language which hasn't a verb,'[2] and swung on with 'the slowest poem in the English language', 'the quickest poem in the English language' following after it, all set pieces produced on every occasion. Stephens said that when reciting poetry to Yeats he had to close his eyes and recite two poems quickly one after the other, or Yeats on catching his attention would start reciting several of his own and never leave the floor.

In his comments as to how poetry should be read Stephens said that the most important thing was a sense of rubato. He also deplored the fact that some people adopt an 'indeterminate or neutral gear when speaking verse'; they employ, he said, a uniform system of speech for every poem and they make it seem as if all poetry is written by one poet. Understanding words and phrases is not enough. The voice, tone and pace often give no hint of the essence of the verse in which the words and phrases are merely 'carriers and carters'. Where there is 'spiritual incomprehension' the reader of a poem kills the poem he is reading.

> The speaker of verse must be exceedingly wide awake, and further is to take scrupulous care of thought, its emotion, its pace and its music. He has only one voice to do all this with and he must do all this effortlessly; and he must make it all to live, and be, and be lovely, and sing.

He grouped verse into three sections, each kind demanding different speech adjustment and attack. The epic must be

---

[1] 'One Afternoon with James Stephens' (*Irish Writing*), March 1951.
[2] 'The Main-Deep'.

uttered in a fashion 'approximating to gravely modulated speech'. The lyrical form 'without being song approximates to a singing'. Finally there is an intermediate form which is come to by a subtle balancing of phrase against phrase, and this guided James Stephens's own method of versification in the last books of poetry. The epic form did not in fact concern him and he wrote no epic poetry, nor did he read the work of epic poets in his recitals. But the two other forms correspond to the song-verse and speech-verse which MacDonagh described in his book on Thomas Campion; with the difference, however, that Stephens put his conversational style not on a level with speech-verse, but somewhere between the lyrical, or musically chanted, poem, and the epic style.

In November 1947, he read 'To the Queen of the Bees' in his broadcast, one of his favourite pieces for recitation. The words were separated and sometimes sounded jerky. He lingered on the 'ss' of 'message' and the 'f' in 'of', and his mellow and distinctive voice balanced phrase against phrase with a definite break between each one. (See diagram on next page.) Here the long slur marks attempt to represent the rising and falling of Stephens's voice and the vertical lines represent his pauses, the double lines showing a longer pause. Hyphens indicate an equal weight on each word, which sounded as if they were joined slowly and rhythmically together, and the words written with ⌐— about them were drawn out, Stephens lingering on them as long as he could.

This was his commonest style of recitation. The other is more specialized. The poet was, in Stephens's words, 'as it were talking to himself and meanwhile singing'. The incantations were based on three notes. C was the dominant one: D (above it) was employed to vary the emotion, while A (below) relieved the monotony occasionally. The long syllables of the line attracted the tone of each note, and weak syllables fitted between them rhythmically. Stephens added a note to two of his poems in *A Poetry Recital* with instructions for their reading. He intended 'His Will' to be read as follows: 'The letters marked with an accent are to be prolonged for as long as it is possible to sound them. Count two beats of that duration at the end of each line, and for the silences between each verse. These sounds and silences are to be considered as one rhythmic

M

Bee! ‖ Tell me, ‖ whence-do-you come? ‖

Ten fields away, ‖ twenty perhaps, ‖

Have heard your hum,

If you are from the North, | you may

Have passed my mother's-roof of straw

Upon your way.

If you are from the South, | you should—

Have seen a little cottage | just—

Inside a wood.

And should you go back that way, | please |

Carry a message | to the house |

Among the trees.

Say— ‖ that I'll meet her at the rock—

Behind the stream,—this very night |

At eight o'clock.

And ask your queen, | when you get home, |

To send my queen—the present of— |

A honeycomb.

166

utterance.' 'Away! Far Away!' was to be treated in the same manner, the accented letters being sounded for as long as possible, but four beats replaced the former two at the end of each verse. With it he gave more indication as to the function of unaccented syllables. 'Unmarked words and phrases are to be said quickly, and ended sharply. All line endings and verse endings, or silences, are to be well held'. The counting of the beats can almost be heard in Stephens's reading of 'The Main-Deep'.

Unlike A.E. and Yeats, Stephens made his phrases full of music and rhythm. So the rhythm of each verse in 'Cadence', when he read it, could be transcribed thus:

See the   mo-ther Running to her   child How   sweet she   goes!

The first and third verses are based mainly on C, the second verse on D. In 'Sarasvati', he employed the same rhythm and melody, though, even if he intended that it should be so, it was never an impersonal way of verse speaking; here the first line was merely spoken, and gradually his emotion was aroused, and a trancelike incantation replaced his normal style of chanting.

For an example it is interesting to linger for a moment on a complete poem and imagine it as it was chanted by Stephens in his individual manner, in his rich melodious voice, as his hand, arms and whole physique moulded each word and phrase; one observer wrote that he at one point found it necessary to jump out of his chair 'to give the sentence all the physical height he could muster'.

The small, green leaf
Fell down from the tree:

And the great oak tree
Fell down from the cliff:

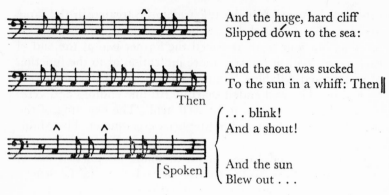

And the huge, hard cliff
Slipped dówn to the sea:

And the sea was sucked
To the sun in a whiff: Then‖

. . . blink!
And a shout!

And the sun
Blew out . . .

His rhythm was very definite, starting slowly, then working steadily and with increasing speed to the climax:

Blínk ‖ and a shóut ‖ and the sún | bléw | oút . . .

In his broadcasts Stephens at last put into words and on record the theories he held about poetry and which he had developed during his friendship with A.E. Some perhaps were originally A.E.'s ideas, but Stephens spread them abroad. He felt that poetry was the most private of the arts and must reserve itself for the devotion of a select group, that it must not lower its tone by speaking to the masses. On the other hand, he feared that beauty might be sacrificed to intellect and therefore he denied that the intellectual content of a poem was of any importance whatever. Enlarging on this he compared poetry with prose, which for him was a method of communication. Poetry, he said, was communion; and not only was the poet dedicated, but any one who wished to read a poem must approach it with awe and a sense of privilege. For the poet may withold nothing whatever there. So sacred is the medium that no lie may be perpetrated in it. 'In the work of every good artist a secret is told', Stephens had written in 1912.

Subtly or boldly the Land of Heart's Desire is indicated, and almost all poems and pictures which are not mere exercises in technique are records of an adventure in quest of the Golden Age . . . From every good artist's work his secret may be guessed.

And poetry must be impersonal or it is bad, for, withdrawn in a transcending vision, it is 'too aery and too incurious' to bother with any man's personal hopes or fears and ambitions. The intellectual content and verbal sense of poetry is of no concern, for the effort is to make music out of thoughts, and the thoughts themselves are of a relative unimportance. So Stephens's early reverence for Imagination, the divine Los, was unshaken during his life. It was what the form of the poem and what the individual words *suggest* that was of prime importance to his mind, for the power of recreating some unique, perhaps mystical, experience belonged to the poet alone.

The subjects of 'real' poetry Stephens used to say are the universal commonplaces, God, and Nature, and Beauty, and the poet must dedicate himself to these and so intensify life for his readers. Poetry is inextricably bound up with man's life:

The mind of man, perpetually dwelling upon itself; perpetually astonished and delighted and affrighted at its own infinity; endlessly discovering, discarding and recreating all that it can hope or imagine, or (which is the same thing) desire, is the subject matter for a poet,

he wrote, and all that a poet must aspire to in his writing is to be simple, sensuous and passionate. The poet must not instruct or entertain. He had no artistic message, because we know and have experienced as much as he, but his gift is to liven our perceptions and to enable us to realize depths in ourselves which we had not apprehended before.

However, assuming a facility for music and literary expression, and a natural comprehension, sympathy and wisdom, the poet must still apply himself diligently to his art: Stephens was not letting himself or anyone else get away easily. For poetry is a craft, and the poet must serve his apprenticeship as well as any other craftsman. Again his ideas were grounded on what he had written so long before at the beginning of his career in 1907.

He must not sing at the touching of a button, but with pain and the sweat of his brow, the way all good work is done. The Muse must be wooed with the passion of a lover . . . Let our poet sing loudly . . . When you sing a war song, howl like a wolf; when you sing a live song, let the girl hear you. Sing of God and Man and sing greatly . . . Sing the woe of the hunted rabbit when his legs begin to fail, and he hears the toothed devil close behind; and sing, too, the joy of the dog when he leaps and feels the red, warm tide flush his throat.

Stephens dedicated himself seriously. He was not alone in this for many of his views were commonly held in Dublin at the beginning of the century; but none clung to them with such passionate intensity as Stephens did. In a talk on G. K. Chesterton, he called poetry 'the practice of the presence of God', and he adopted A.E.'s dictum and practised it to the exclusion of lighter verses in his late work. True poetry, he wrote, is born on the Mount of Transfiguration.

Unless at some point in a poem this transformation of matter takes place, the work is temporary and merely a poetic note on the mode of thinking and feeling the day when it was composed.

He was convinced that his poetry was dictated to him, that he merely acted as an ananuensis, and that his job was to tidy up the verse-form and expression. The poet's aim is *ecstasy*, his term for the essence of life; and the poet

> . . . cannot too much sing
> The heaven, the earth, the everything.

While he could at last formulate his theories on the art of poetry it was in a way his method of signing off; for Stephens published no more poetry after this, though he broadcast up to the end of his life, and the only verse he wrote were the scraps he jotted in the flyleaves of the books he was reading. He read a great deal while he was in the Chapel and now became interested in what Kot had done.

16 March 1941

Dear Kot.

. . . Do you remember telling me, some time ago, that you had been rereading Tolstoi; & that some particular short story of his, which you had already read twenty times, had quite suddenly revealed itself to you, so that you saw a new story, & a new Tolstoi, & a new Kot. Well I've just got a book 'Twenty Three Stories', by Tol. published Oxford Un. Press trans. Louise & Aylmer Mand. I think you said (or imagine) that your

story was in such a collection. Could you tell me its name again.
I've read a few of these. How good he is! And how he makes our
story-writers seem mean & unfortunate!

In August he wrote to say that he had 'one minute ago,
bought a sixpenny of Russian story' under Koteliansky's name,
and he wished that Kot had written a long introduction, and
three days later, 25 August 1941, a letter came praising the
first story 'Ribnikov'. He would next turn to the River of Life.
But he was sorry not to have seen Koteliansky:

> When I was in town B.B.C.'ing there was never an opportunity
> of getting in touch with you. I'd get in at one o'c. Begin
> rehearsals at 2. Keep at it till six. have a drink. Rehearse again
> at 7 o'c. Give the stuff at 8 o'c. Get away at 8.30. Get some food.
> Get home before Blackout about 9.30, or 10, & be away next
> morning by the 10 o'c train. And I couldn't tell you I was
> coming, for I never know if the 1 o'c train got in at 1 or at half 2.
> And there was always the devil in it, and the devil of a fog in it
> too. Those 3 to 4 hours of crowded travelling are tiresome, but I
> like to do them because I like the fee, and need it too. Down
> here we never see one soul in a month. We are far away in the
> wilds, 8 miles from a station. Every now & then we see Wm. &
> Alice Rothenstein, & thats about all our seeing. Grub is scarce,
> cigarettes are even scarcer, but the countryside (immediately
> outside of our door, that is) is interesting, even lovely, the
> weather rotten. A boche, or two, or five, groans over us every
> night. And life's not worth living. I cant write, & wish I never
> had to write again; and wish, too that we had never left London.
> On each trip that I made to London I carried back with me a
> bagful of books, mostly Buddhist things. Are you keeping well?
> We had good talks together. Remember me to Mr. & Mrs.
> Julian Huxley if you see them, & to whoever else remembers me.

There were moments of deep depression such as these, but
there were moments of enthusiasm too, for just a few days after
this he wrote a note to Kot to congratulate him on his book:

> Dear Kot. This is only a word to say I've finished the short
> stories, & that they are beautifully written, except the first two
> which, tho' good, are not as good as the others. I note you have
> also a book of plays Penguined. I was very interested in those
> stories, & especially interested to see how your English moved
> under a pen.

Koteliansky, too, shared any pieces of poetry that appeared.
In December, on St. Stephen's Day, Stephens wrote to him:

Here is a bit of a poem I got the other day. I'm only sending
it to wish you a happy New Year—

> Soul and sense are gone from me
> And I am but a shape of grief,
> For this morning did I see
> Loveliness beyond belief.
>
> In the twinkle of the morn,
> On the hillside, in the dew,
> I a hoping heart did warn
> —Loveliness is not for you.
>
> All that morn can bring will fall
> In an afternoon away,
> And the night will drowse it all
> In the dream of yesterday—
>
> So the mind admonisheth!
> But the heart, that hopeing thing,
> Thinks it will not die the death,
> —Hopes against admonishing!

Stephens continued to broadcast after the War when they
had returned to London. He told stories and read verse, he
spoke about his friends in Dublin, A.E., Yeats, Joyce, Shaw,
and MacKenna, and he attempted some critical appreciation,
speaking on Blake, of course, and on Donne, and on Thomas
Moore. Then there were talks on talkers and the art of talking,
and talks on poetry and how to write it. The B.B.C. also
arranged readings from *The Crock of Gold* which were more
successful than any of his broadcasts and are still remembered
for their individuality and charm.

Though he had no money worries since he had been put on
the British Civil Pension List in 1942, when he was offered the
degree of Doctor of Literature by Dublin University his first
impulse was to refuse as he felt he could not afford the fare and
the expense that the journey to Dublin would entail. However,
he received a payment from the Royal Bounty Fund on 30 June
1947, and the degree was conferred in the following October,

when he spent a week in his old haunts. 'We have of recent years,' said the orator,

> honoured two Irish poets, William Butler Yeats and James Sullivan Starkey. Today we are followed by a third, JAMES STEPHENS, whose genius is so varied that some critics compare him with Aeschylus, some with Milton, while others regard his gift as mainly, if not entirely, lyric. When expert opinion is so divided, what wonder that a Public Orator should lose his bearings: *Stat et incertus qua sit sibi, nescit eundum.*
> But it may at least be safely said that
> Howe'er posterity shall view these deeds JAMES STEPHENS will always have a place among the Muses' chief priests. In his presentation of the immensities—Eternity, Space, Force—in his picture of the Lord walking in the deserted garden, in his account of what Thomas said in a pub about the anger of the Almighty 'he passes beyond what is simply human and becomes a voice for the Spirit of Poetry'; *musas ipsas audire videaris,* of prose writers too, as everybody knows, he is in the first rank. It is scarcely necessary to cite *The Demi-Gods, The Charwoman's Daughter* and the most widely known perhaps of all his works, *The Crock of Gold.* To one so eminent the most enthusiastic applause is due.[1].

So James Stephens received intellectual recognition of his genius, a fitting close to his career as a writer.

As soon as he returned to England he had to undergo an operation, and after this his friends saw him rarely and he shunned company, being unfit for much excitement. On 11 June 1950, 'Childhood Days', a charming performance in his best form, which extolled all that in which a child delights, was recorded. It was his last broadcast.

---

[1] Oration translated by Oliver St. John Gogarty. (*Colby Library Quarterly*), March 1961.

XII

Conclusion

'How many men have loved you? Women, yes; but I am not
talking about sexual love. How many men have loved you?'
Oliver St. John Gogarty: James Stephens.
From Colby Library Quarterly, March 1961

IT is easy to expatiate on Stephens's qualities as a writer, on his
attractive personality, the individualism and the whimsy; the
love of exaggeration and the fantastic stories; the tendency to
treat serious matters with apparent levity; the ability to talk for
hours on any subject. But when judging him in the general
context of English Literature one cannot deny that his output
was small for a writer of eminence—half a dozen 'novels', two
books of short stories and a volume of his collected poems. It is
rather unfortunate that he matured early as a writer, for, having
adopted an ideal philosophy at the beginning of his career, his
work had little chance to develop. There is no history of an
internal struggle and resultant triumph.

Nevertheless, he has proved himself worthy of a permanent
place in English literature. In a world grown pessimistic after
the downfall of established customs he offered ultimate values
where human ones were fast becoming standard. He exalted the
spirit of literature rather than the letter, preaching that the
author has a spiritual duty as well as an artistic one. 'Success
depends on the variety of one's inner life' was his dictum; and
he reminded the critic, in 'An Essay in Cubes', that he 'is not
celebrating a man, but a soul'. His career as a writer is the
story of the development of this inner life. His religious sensitivity was fortunately combined with a talent for artistic
expression, and he had a distinct advantage in his large and
aptly chosen vocabulary, the result of omnivorous reading, so
that he could range from a leisurely narrative to an incantatory

prose in *The Crock of Gold*; and the impersonal tones of *Here Are Ladies*, where he preoccupied himself with the rambling of the individual's thoughts, and the dramatic opening paragraphs of *The Demi-Gods* were equally his own. His poetic insight displayed itself in the gift of remembering what happened in the flush of a moment and recreating the full richness of an experience directly instead of by intimation.

His limitation was that as a writer he stood alone; he founded no school of writing and the threads of tradition which he picked up were absorbed into a style that was his and inimitable. His practice of raising the commonplace into the realm of the unknown has caused his work to be branded as trivial, pastoral and mere fantasy; but the terms 'fantasy' and 'pastoral' are inaccurate, and confining if they mean that he is to be grouped with writers of fantasy in English and American literature such as Thurber, Tolkien or Welty. In *The Crock of Gold* he did view life from one angle. The setting is idealized, with the artificiality of a Chinese garden. Similarly, in *The Charwoman's Daughter*, though Mary has to go to work as a charwoman, the scrubbing brush is not the real part of her life, nor is it what her mother has brought her up to expect. Her experiences and the ideas that develop in her mind are the important part of existence. She lives, removed from the world, in a dream. But the term fantasy is erroneous in that the part of her which lives in the dream is essentially human and not idealized. Stephens simply disregarded the concrete world in order to give more space to fundamental questions about the universe.

His characters are independently concerned with spiritual ideas. Mrs. Makebelieve sees even her working life in terms of an ultimate reality and not as a relationship of employee and employer. The Philosopher, like her, has never occupied himself with mundane affairs, but deals with the investigation of what lies beyond our experience and knowledge. Here, however, Stephens showed his down-to-earth humour in the wit arising out of this attitude concerning everyday matters, as for instance the theft of the washboard. Even Meehawl MacMurrachu lives in this enlarged world of supernatural perceptions, where fairies also look to ultimate reality for the answer to problems. It is this present world translated into spiritual terms, and physical and intellectual problems are set beside the supernatural. Those who live in the human conventional world are represented throughout Stephens's work by the Policeman, who has no curiosity or wonder, but is solely interested in the Law and how to prevent the breach of it. In *The Demi-Gods* he attempted to move the centre of the idealized world of *The Crock of Gold* back to the everyday world he knew, and, while trying to explain Patsy MacCann's movements in ultimate terms, found a place for the archangels round the tinkers' fire, and on the hunt for food each day. He saw the supernatural in relation to what humans actually experience. In the years that followed his ideas developed, and finally, as his philosophy reached a satisfactory conclusion, his interest rested in the concrete world of human relationships which he had taken for granted before, and he became concerned with psychological problems.

His manner of writing owed much to his familiarity with a world beyond our perceptions. His capricious wit never became malicious, though in a rare case he might chastise something he believed was wrong very severely, and its character often persuaded his readers that what he had to say was not to be taken seriously:

> When the war was finished the English loss did not total nineteen thousand men, but Ireland mourned for over fifty thousand and these fifty thousand were not all killed in battle. They were hunted through the mountains and the glens. They were bayonetted in the home, the field and the church. They were flogged and pitch-capped and hung and cut down again. They were quarter-hung and half-hung, and three-quarters hung and finally hung. And if there is any truth in the Buddhist doctrine of reincarnation these men were eminently fitted to be giraffes in the next world through the neck stretching they got in this one . . .

So he described the fate of the insurgents in the rebellion of 1798, in an article published in *Sinn Féin*, giving strength to his words with this rueful humour. He had a general habit of jesting about the most serious things and about what is most deeply believed in, and to many people it was mere flippancy.

The habit of not taking himself too seriously meant that most absurd statements might be ventured, for it was likely that they would be contradicted straight away; and since human criteria of conduct were ignored in the notions of an indefinable Eternity, there was no standard by which the importance of an idea or the significance of an event might be precisely measured. In fact his exaggerations were generally based on the truth. The practice was to start with a logical statement, but to give it emphasis by isolating it, and this was achieved by setting it above its fellows. Yeats, MacKenna and A.E. also tended to make simple events seem more important and significant by this exaggeration; and his bombastic claim to be the greatest living prose writer was paralleled by Yeats's habit of austere self-dramatization. Stephens was famous in Dublin for the ability to create an epic out of a fight between a beetle and a cockroach. Any additional trimming to a tale was regarded by its audience as an improvement, and a story was enhanced by an impish sense of fun or sometimes a witty contrariness.

In an age when imagination tends to be ousted by scientific thought the quality of realism has stood Irish writers in good stead, and one of their virtues is a hard-boiled ability to describe events without any colouring of emotion. Yeats noticed, in a letter to Florence Farr, that it was a native characteristic that the writers of Ireland who come from the mass of the people 'have more reason than fantasy. It is the other way with those who come from the leisured classes'. This, of course, applies to every land, but it is marked in the writing of the Irish literary renaissance at the beginning of this century, and an example is witnessed in the total dissimilarity of Yeats's and Colum's work of that time. A taste for realism is evident in other ways too. Joyce made sure his references were exact, while Liam O'Flaherty and Frank O'Connor describe situations minutely and with complete objectivity. Stephens also treated his characters with what O Faracháin called 'cold, appalling commonsense'. His people were approached as real characters capable of directing the action of his tales. To him there was no distinction of class or money, but people were accepted on their merits for what they were themselves. The Philosopher could sit down to eat with a farmer's wife without embarrassment.

He differed from the other Irish writers of his generation, however, in that, in his frank disregard of social position, he similarly wished to make friends with heavenly bodies, and so archangel sups with tinker, Angus Óg finds a shepherd-girl for a wife, and a leprechaun teaches two children how to play leap-frog. O'Flaherty has written some delightful and sympathetic stories about animals, but only Stephens could imagine himself as a spider, or bring a donkey, on terms of equality, into the same circle as human beings. It was an unsentimental attitude, resulting from 'humanizing' the characters, whether divine or bestial, and then letting them express themselves as they wished. All beings were, to him, on an equal plane; they were all filled with an essential common spirit which, when the first shyness had been conquered, gave rise to a healthy curiosity and a respect for other people.

The only way in which he could have influenced the literary trend of his country was by his establishment of an oral technique in prose and verse and such a development was, in spite of him, inevitable. His manner too, was individual. In general, a young writer experiments and imitates in an attempt to reach a style conducive to his artistic method, and, having perfected it, he plays, as it were, on an instrument. The author who has a good style may be compared with the gentleman who has cultivated manners. Stephens differed in that his style was literally himself. It was his own personality, and he had no need to train his pen because his way of speech was created already. *The Demi-Gods* might have been his greatest book had it not been marred by the self-consciousness his sojourn in Paris gave him; and it is by *The Crock of Gold* and *Irish Fairy Tales*, the highest achievements of his imaginative realism, that his name will be remembered.

The final years were very sad; he cut himself off from everyone he knew, feeling an alien atmosphere in the post-war world. He was worn out with illness. He preferred to be by himself and he would spend the hours when he was in good health wandering in a lonely way about London bookshops, a tiny, shabbily clad figure in a tweed suit, with long whiskery threads hanging down where the elbow had been worn through. One day his disreputable appearance caused quite a stir in Regent Street. Coming in the opposite direction he recognized Lady Beatrice Glenavy, he revived with joy and he rushed forward to embrace her. A friend of Lady Glenavy's with her, who did not know Stephens, was horrified to see the tiny tramp swarming up her and was about to call the police when to his relief an introduction explained everything.[1] He was always getting lost in London, and on these occasions he said, he would make for Piccadilly Circus, the only place he could find, and he would take a taxi from Piccadilly to the required destination. Mrs. Stephens would fetch him home in the evening in the car.

Ill-health was chronic, and another bout of double-pneumonia took away much of the writer's energy. Several times he collapsed. The ulcers in his stomach sometimes prevented him from eating for days on end. The year before his death he collapsed in the street and he was taken to St. George's Hospital for treatment.

His last appearance in public was in London at an event run by the Department of External Affairs. The film about W. B. Yeats was being shown at a cinema in Oxford Street. Stephens was seen going into the cinema, arm-in-arm with John Dulanty, and they were quoting poetry to one another. During the film they were heard still quoting softly to each other in the dark.

In July 1950 Kees Van Hoek was preparing an article on Stephens for *The Irish Times*[2] and visited him in Kingsbury. The poet was recovering from an operation for gastric ulcers and was very weak, but from the moment that he entered the room in his baggy suit, with the eye-glass incongruously staring about him, telling stories of the people he had known and of Dublin, reciting Joyce and his own work, he took command. There were only 'a few minutes of my three hours with him,' wrote Van Hoek, 'when his hands were not shaping, his arms moulding, his features modelling the words he was speaking', and at one point he impishily answered a bird in its own language of song. But suddenly he was tired and could do no more. Austin Clarke has also mentioned an amusing supper party at the Café Royal later that year when Stephens was in excellent form. Three weeks later he was dead.

'How many men have loved you?', Stephens asked St. John Gogarty. Winning the love of fellow men was his estimate of success in life; and there is no doubt that he himself was a resounding success. Few people have lived of whom no ill can be recalled and who are yet remembered for their individuality and exciting and entertaining company.

[1] Lady Glenavy.
[2] *Irish Times*, Saturday, 22 July 1950.

Those who knew him well realized that he was flagging in those last years. When asked to tell a story he would start the tale of the three hermits who lived in the desert. At the end of the first year the first hermit remarked: 'It is very quiet here'; the second hermit replied, at the end of the following year, 'it is', and one year later the third hermit burst out: 'Will you all keep quiet!' Stephens related it with all of his mastery, but it was A.E.'s story, and for that reason had a tinge of pathos. Similarly he would recite 'The Main-Deep', calling it his newest poem. But he still had moments of his former inspiration when in the company of those who stimulated him and prompted his resources by supplying rejoinders of their own. For a man who loved to feel he was the centre of attention, permanent life on a stage had encouraged mental stagnation.

James Stephens died appropriately enough, and as in his whimsy he would have wished, on St. Stephen's Day. The Stephenses were in the habit of visiting Iris and her husband on Christmas Day for dinner, but Stephens had fallen on the stairs and remained indoors as he felt unwell; and he passed the day wandering about the house and reading a little. Mrs. Stephens read some La Fontaine before they retired for the night. Early next morning he died. He was buried in Kingsbury Old Graveyard, in North London, on a bitterly cold day, near his son. The funeral was quiet, attended by about a dozen people. Besides his immediate family, Mr. John Dulanty, the late Ambassador, with whom he had long standing friendship, came. Mr. Harold Macmillan, later Prime Minister, represented his publishers, and Mr. Michael Noyk, a solicitor friend of his from Dublin, and four Irish journalists were there too.

He would have wished that his end should seem quiet, for it was not finality for him. He always believed that he would be born again. However a fortnight later, on Thursday, 25 January 1951, his immediate loss was admitted by the vast numbers who attended the Memorial Service in St. Martin-in-the-Fields.

> Put on diadem and wing
> —Death and worm
> Put nobly on—
> Thirst shall come with you
> To sing:

Conclusion

Grief can be depended on:
Those with you are one,
And ye
Are beauty, truth, and victory.[1]

[1] 'In Grey Air'. *Collected Poems*, p. 342.

181

Bibliography

I. PUBLICATIONS OF JAMES STEPHENS

1908   *Where the demons grin.* A Broadside. Cuala Press, Dublin.

1909   *Why Tomas Cam Was Grumpy.* A Broadside. Cuala Press, Dublin.
      Insurrections. Maunsel & Co., Dublin.

1910   *The Adventures of Seumas Beg: The Visit from Abroad.* A Broadside. Cuala Press, Dublin.
      The Adventures of Seumas Beg: In the Orchard. A Broadside. Cuala Press, Dublin.
      The Adventures of Seumas Beg: Treasure Trove. A Broadside. Cuala Press, Dublin.
      The Spy. A Broadside. Cuala Press, Dublin.

1912   *The Hill of Vision.* Maunsel & Co., Dublin.
      The Charwoman's Daughter. Macmillan & Co., London.
      The Crock of Gold. Macmillan & Co., London.

1913   *Five New Poems.* Flying Fame Chapbooks, London.
      Here Are Ladies. Macmillan & Co., London.

1914   *The Demi-Gods.* Macmillan & Co., London.

1915   *Songs From the Clay.* Macmillan & Co., London.
      The Adventures of Seumas Beg. The Rocky Road to Dublin. Macmillan & Co., London.

1916   *The Insurrection in Dublin.* Maunsel & Co., Dublin & London.
      Green Branches. Maunsel & Co., Dublin & London.

1918   *Reincarnations.* Macmillan & Co., London.
      Hunger: a Dublin Story, by James Esse. Candle Press, Dublin.

1920   *Irish Fairy Tales.* Macmillan & Co., London.
      The Year's at the Spring. An anthology of recent poetry compiled by L. D'O Walters. (To this James Stephens contributed 'Check', 'When the Leaves Fall'.) London.

1922   *Arthur Griffith.* Wilson, Hartnell & Co., Dublin.

1923   *Deirdre.* Macmillan & Co. London.

1924   *In the Land of Youth.* Macmillan, London & New York.
      Little Things. Kentucky.

1925   *Christmas in Freelands.* Kentucky.
      A Poetry Recital. Macmillan & Co., London.

1926 *Collected Poems.* Macmillan & Co., London.
   The Oxford Book of Modern Verse, 1892–1925. Chosen by
   W. B. Yeats. (To this Stephens contributed 'Deirdre',
   'Blue Blood', 'A Glass of Beer', 'Egan O'Rahilly', 'Inis
   Fal', 'The Rivals', 'In the Night', 'The Main-Deep'.)
   London.
1928 *On Prose and Verse.* New York.
   Etched in Moonlight. Macmillan & Co., London.
1929 *The Outcast.* Faber & Faber, London.
   The Symbol Song. New York.
   Julia Elizabeth, a comedy in one act. New York.
   Theme and Variations. Fountain Press, New York.
1931 *Strict Joy.* Macmillan & Co., London.
1935 *The Fifteen Acres.* A Broadside. Cuala Press, Dublin.
1937 *Broadsides. A Collection of New Irish and English Songs,* edited
   by Dorothy Wellesley and W. B. Yeats. Cuala Press,
   Dublin. (To this Stephens contributed 'The Main-Deep'
   and 'The Rivals'.)
1938 *Kings and the Moon.* Macmillan & Co., London.
1954 *Collected Poems* (second edition, with added material).
   Macmillan & Co., London
1957 *Modern Irish Short Stories.* Selected with an introduction by
   Frank O'Connor. The World's Classics. By Stephens: 'A
   Rhinoceros, Some Ladies and a Horse'.

II. CONTRIBUTIONS BY JAMES STEPHENS TO PERIODICALS

1905 'The Greatest Miracle.' *United Irishman,* 16 Sept.
1907 'The Seoinin.' *Sinn Féin,* 20 April.
   'Builders.' ibid, 11 May.
   'Patriotism and Parochial Politics.' ibid., 25 May.
   'Irish Englishmen.' ibid., 1 June.
   'Poetry.' ibid., 22 June.
   'Nature ag Labhairt.' ibid., 29 June.
   'The Song of Ossian.' ibid., 3 Aug.
   'Mrs. Maurice M'Quillan.' ibid., 17 Aug.
   'The Stranger.' ibid., 7 Sept.
   'Tattered Thoughts.' ibid., 5 Oct.
   'Mrs. Jerry Gorman.' ibid., 2 Nov.
   'Miss Arabella Hennessy.' ibid., 21 Dec.
1908 'To Mr. George Birmingham's "Asses".' An Epistle. ibid.,
   4 Jan.
   'Mrs. Larry Tracy.' ibid., 4 Jan.

'The Rebel.' *Sinn Féin*, 18 Jan.
'Another Rebel.' ibid., 1 Feb.
'Old Mrs. Hannigan.' ibid., 29 Feb.
'The Insurrection of '98.' ibid., 21 March.
'Success.' ibid., 28 March.
'Miss Kathleen Raftery.' ibid., 10 Oct.
'So Early in the Morning O.' ibid., 24 Oct.
'As Autumn Ends.' ibid., 19 Dec.
'The Watcher.' ibid., 26 Dec.

1909 'A November Ride.' ibid., 9 Jan.
'The Old Philosopher on Washing.' ibid., 16 Jan.
'The Old Philosopher on Going to Bed.' ibid., 30 Jan.
'The Old Philosopher on Shaving.' ibid., 6 Feb.
'The Old Philosopher on Eating.' ibid., 13 Feb.
'Translations (After Sappho): I. Midnight. II. To a Rich Lady.' ibid., 29 May.
'Translations (After Sappho): Afterwards.' ibid., 5 June.
'Translations (After Sappho): I. Query. II. Snow Time.' ibid., 19 June.
'The Old Philosopher on Drinking.' ibid., 26 June.
'Translations (After Sappho): Patience at the Loom.' ibid., 10 July.
'The Old Philosopher on Smoking.' ibid., 4 Sept.
'The Old Philosopher on the Viceregal Microbe.' ibid., 11 Sept.
'The Old Philosopher on Education.' ibid., 18 Sept.
'The Old Philosopher on Policemen: On the North Pole.' ibid., 25 Sept.
'The Old Philosopher on Language.' ibid., 2 Oct.
'Imagination.' ibid., 16 Oct.

1910 'King Guaire.' ibid., 12 Feb.
'Oisín and Niamh.' ibid., 26 Feb.
'The Guests.' ibid., 12 March.
'Peadar Og Goes Courting.' ibid., 16 April.
'Irish Idiosyncrasies.' ibid., 7 May.
'October.' ibid., 21 May.
'Good and Evil.' ibid., 21 May.
'Summer.' ibid., 18 June.
'Down by the Moat.' Ibid., 25 June.
'Thomas Muskerry.' ibid., 16 July.
'The Breath of Life.' ibid., 6 Aug.
'The Fairy Boy.' ibid., 20 Aug.
'On Politeness.' ibid., 17 Sept.

'Love.' *Sinn Féin,* 1 Oct.

'Facts.' ibid., 1 Oct.

'Caricatures.' ibid., 22 Oct.

'A Reply to an Open Letter.' ibid., 5 Nov.

'Little Lady.' *Open Window,* Nov.

'Holiday.' ibid.

'Epithalamium.' *Sinn Féin,* 26 Nov.

1911 'In the Poppy Field.' *Irish Review,* March.

'Bessie Bobtail.' ibid., April.

'Duty.' *Nash's Magazine,* Oct.

1912 'Mac Dhoul.' *Irish Review,* Jan.

'The Populace Mind.' *Irish Citizen,* 1 June, 8 June, 15 June, 22 June.

'Eight Poems' (with an introductory note by Richard Aldington). *Poetry Review,* June.

'An Adventure of Seumas Beg.' *Irish Review,* June.

'December.' *Sinn Féin,* 21 Dec.

'The Appointment.' ibid., 21 Dec.

1913 'The Daisies.' *Irish Review,* Jan.

'The Reason.' ibid., May.

'Jealousy.' ibid., July.

'Enter Mr. James Stephens.' *New Age,* 20 Nov.

'Come Off that Fence!' *Irish Worker,* 13 Dec.

1914 'Four Poems. I. Deirdre. II. The Voice of God. III. The Centaurs. IV. In the Dark.' *Irish Review,* April.

1915 'Affirmations. A Reply to an article by Ezra Pound.' *New Age,* 18 March.

'Charity.' *Collier's Magazine,* 22 May.

'The Sad Shepherd.' ibid., 3 July.

'Proud Mountains.' ibid., 14 Aug.

'The End of "Romanticism" A Reply to an article by Ramiro de Maeztu.' ibid., 30 Sept.

'The Fur Coat.' *New Ireland,* 2 Oct.

'Peace in War Time.' *Collier's Magazine,* 11 Dec.

1916 'God Bless the Work.' *New Ireland,* 22 April.

'An Open Letter to Shaw.' *New Age,* 4 May.

1917 'Anthology: Mary Hynes. Nancy Walsh.' *New Ireland,* 7 July.

'Anthology: Mary Ruane. Anthony O'Daly.' ibid., 14 July.

'Anthology: Peggy Mitchell. William O'Kelly.' ibid., 21 July.

'Anthology: Eileen, Diarmaid and Teig. The Coolun.' ibid., 28 July.

'Anthology: The Red Man's Wife. Nancy Walsh.' ibid., 4 Aug.

Bibliography

'Anthology: Clan Cartie.' *New Ireland*, 11 Aug.
'To Joachim du Bellay.' ibid., 25 Aug.
'Anthology: Egan O'Rahilly. Righteous Anger.' ibid., 27 Oct.
'Anthology: The Geraldine's Cloak.' ibid., 3 Nov.
'Anthology: Blue Blood.' ibid., 10 Nov.
'Anthology: Plus Ça Change.' ibid., 17 Nov.
'Anthology: Inis Fail.' ibid., 1 Dec.
'Anthology: O Dell.' ibid., 8 Dec.
'Anthology: Skim-milk. The County Mayo.' ibid., 22 Dec.

1918 'Three sketches.' *Century Magazine*, Sept.

1919 'Mythology. Quaint Tales of Origination.' The Cult of Death. *The Times*, 4 Nov.

1922 'Wind and Tree.' *American Bookman* (N.Y.), May–Aug.
'Literature and Life: An Interview with James Stephens by James Esse.' *Irish Statesman*, 22 Sept.
'Arthur Griffith: Four Appreciations. I. Alice Stopford Green. II. James Stephens. III. Robert M. Henry. IV. P. S. O'Hegarty.' *Studies*, Sept.

1925 'Christmas in Freelands.' *Irish Statesman*, 26 Dec.

1928 'The Irish Situation. For St. Patrick's Day.' *Radio Times*, 9 March.

1930 'America's Place in History. A conversation between James Stephens, Miss Mary Crowley and Dr. James Murphy.' *Forum*, Feb.

1934 'An Irish Prophecy.' ibid., Aug,

1935 'The Passing of AE.' *Observer*, 21 July.

III. CRITICISM BY JAMES STEPHENS

1909 'Love's Mendicant.' Review of Susan L. Mitchell's *The Living Chalice*. *Sinn Féin*, 17 July.

1910 'A New Book by Seumas O'Sullivan.' Review of *The Earth Lover and Other Verses*. ibid., 15 Jan.
'Decadence.' *The Hours of Fiametta* by Rachel A. Taylor reviewed. ibid., 8 Oct.
'A Gaelic League Art Exhibition.' A review. ibid., 15 Oct.
'Books for Christmas.' *Celtic Wonder Tales* by Ella Young and *Songs of Myself* by Thomas MacDonagh reviewed. ibid., 24 Dec.

1912 *A Western Awakening*. A book of verse by Bligh T. Crosbie reviewed. ibid., 3 Feb.
The Wisdom of the West by James Cousins reviewed. *Irish Review*, April.

Bibliography

'The Irish Year.' Review of *My Irish Year* by Pádraic Colum. *Irish Review*, Aug.

Poems of Love and Earth by John Drinkwater reviewed. *Poetry Review*, Sept.

1914 'An Essay in Cubes.' *English Review*, April–July.

1915 'Letter: James Stephens attacking Ezra Pound.' *New Age*, 18 March.

'Letter: James Stephens attacking Ramiro de Maeztu.' ibid., 7 Oct.

1916 *The Poetical Works of Thomas MacDonagh.* Preface by James Stephens. Dublin.

1922 'An Adventure in Prophecy.' *Atlantic Monthly*, May.

'The Outlook for Literature, with special reference to Ireland.' *Century Magazine*, Oct.

1924 'The Novelist and Final Utterance.' *Irish Statesman*, 12 April.

'Growth in Fiction.' ibid., 27 May.

The Worm Ouroboros by E. R. Eddison reviewed. ibid., 19 July.

Contemporary British Artists by Ambrose McEvoy reviewed. ibid., 2 Aug.

1926 *Ulick and Soracha* by George Moore reviewed. *Observer*, 1 Aug.

1927 *Others Abide* by Humbert Wolfe reviewed. ibid., 18 Sept.

1929 *The Sword in the Soul* by Roger Chauviré, translated by Ernest Boyd with a preface by James Stephens. London, New York, Toronto.

1933 *The English Romantic Poets.* Edited by J. Stephens, Edwin L. Beck, and Royall H. Snow, with an introduction by James Stephens. New York.

1934 *Victorian and Later English Poets.* Edited by J. Stephens, Edwin L. Beck and Royall H. Snow, with an introduction by James Stephens. New York.

Jews in Germany by Joseph Kastein, with a preface by James Stephens. London.

1936 *A Trophy in Arms: Poems 1926–1935* by Ruth Pitter, with a preface by James Stephens. New York.

1939 *Behold This Dreamer* by Walter de la Mare reviewed. *Observer*, 14 May.

IV. B.B.C. BROADCASTS BY JAMES STEPHENS

(Where recordings have been preserved and I have listened to them, I give the date of transmission.)

1937 On Speaking Verse. B.B.C. Recording, 18 May.

(James Stephens reading) 'The Small Green Leaf.' ibid., 1 Sept.

Bibliography

1939   Here's Wishing. *Listener*, 5 Jan.

1941   How Should Poetry Be Read? (A discussion between T. Hunt, C. Day Lewis, R. Nichols, J. Stephens, R. Speaight and F. Compton.) ibid., 22 May.

Must Poetry Make Sense? (A discussion between T. Hunt, J. Stephens, R. Nichols, F. Compton and C. Day Lewis.) ibid., 5 June.

Is Verse-Speaking a Lost Art? (A discussion between J. Stephens, R. Nichols, C. Lacey, G. Thorburn, J. Laurie, V. C. Clinton-Baddeley.) ibid., 12 June.

Does it Stick in Your Throat? (A discussion on the use of the voice between M. Gullan, J. Stephens, R. Nichols, and P. Phillips.) ibid., 24 July.

1942   Yeats and the Telephone. ibid., 22 Jan.

A.E.: A Wonderful Amateur. ibid., 9 April.

1943   Villages I Remember. ibid., 18 March.

He Died Younger Than he was Born. James Stephens on W. B. Yeats. ibid., 17 June.

Two Great Talkers. James Stephens on A.E. and Shaw. ibid., 16 Sept.

1944   Thomas Moore: Champion Minor Poet. ibid., 8 June.

1945   An Irishman's Days. ibid., 22 Feb.

The Story of a Good Dog. ibid., June.

The 'Purest' Poet of Them All. James Stephens on W. Blake. ibid., 6 Sept.

On William Blake. B.B.C. Recording, 8 Oct.

1946   Poetry For Fun. On Poetry and Verse. *Listener*, 7 Feb.

The Chinese were impressed. A story for St. Patrick's Day. ibid., 28 March.

Novels—Dead or Alive? (A discussion between R. Macaulay and J. Stephens.) ibid., 13 June.

Talk and Talkers. ibid., 4 July.

The 'Period' Talent of G. K. Chesterton. ibid., 17 Oct.

The James Joyce I knew. ibid., 24 Oct. B.B.C. Recording, 8 Oct.

1947   A Conversation with George Moore. *Listener*, 16 Jan.

The Prince of Wits: an Appreciation of John Donne. ibid., 23 Jan.

1947   A Poet Speaks: a talk about the writing of poetry. B.B.C. Recording, 3 June.

Living—Whatever That Is. *Listener*, 19 June.

(James Stephens reading) 'The Bee.' B.B.C. Recording, 14 Nov.

Bibliography

1948 A Memory of 'A.E.' *Listener*, 22 Jan.
       Stephen MacKenna: Talker and Philosopher. ibid., 29 Jan.
       No More Peasants. ibid., 26 Aug.
1950 (James Stephens reading from) *The Crock of Gold.* B.B.C.
       Recording, 28 March.
       Childhood Days. ibid., 11 June.

V. MANUSCRIPT MATERIAL CONSULTED

Letters to T. Bodkin, S. S. Koteliansky, E. MacLysaght, Miss H. Mecredy, Mrs. Sleith.

A notebook on Indian philosophy.
Notes and scraps of verse in the books of Stephens's library. } By permission of the late Mrs. Stephens.

Manuscript poem by permission of Professor Sleith.

Typescript of early poems, printed books containing alterations by James Stephens in various ownership.

Photostats of manuscripts and typescripts in New York Public Library.

VI. PUBLICATIONS ABOUT JAMES STEPHENS

Bramsback, B. *James Stephens: a literary and bibliographical study.* Upsala. 1959.

Colby Library Quarterly, March 1961. *A tribute to James Stephens, 1882–1950.*

Friends of the Library of Trinity College, Dublin *Annual Bulletin.* 1955.

Frankenberg, L. *James Stephens: a selection.* New York. 1962.

Frankenberg, L. *James, Seumas & Jacques. Unpublished writings of James Stephens.* London. 1964.

SUGGESTIONS FOR FURTHER READING

A.E. [George Russell]. *Some passages from the letters of A.E. to W. B. Yeats.* Cuala Press, Dublin. 1936.

Bax, Arnold. *Farewell, My Youth.* London. 1943.

Bax, Clifford. *Florence Farr, Bernard Shaw, W. B. Yeats: Letters.* London. 1946.

Boyd, Ernest. *Portraits: Real and Imaginary.* London. 1924.

Carty, J. *Ireland. A documentary record.* (3 vols.). London. 1949, 1951.

Denson, A. (ed.). *Letters from AE.* London. 1961.

Dodds, E. R. *Journal and Letters of Stephen MacKenna.* London. 1936.

Gilbert, S. *James Joyce: Letters.* London. 1957.

Bibliography

Gregory, Lady Augusta. *Our Irish Theatre*. London. 1914.
    Journals, 1916–30. London. 1946.
Gwynn, S. *Irish Literature and Drama*. London. 1936.
Holt, E. *Protest in Arms*. London. 1960.
Hone, Joseph. *W. B. Yeats*, 1865–1939. London. 1942.
Law, Hugh, *Anglo-Irish Literature*. Dublin. 1926.
MacDonagh, T. *Literature in Ireland*. Dublin. 1916.
Moore, G. *Hail and Farewell*. Ave, 1911, Salve, 1912, Vale, 1914.
    London.
O'Casey, Sean. *I Knock at the Door*. London. 1939.
    Drums under the Windows. London. 1945.
    Innisfallen, Fare Thee Well. London. 1949.
O'Faracháin, R. *The Course of Irish Verse in English*. London. 1948.
Ussher, Arland. *Three Great Irishmen: Shaw, Yeats and Joyce*. London.
    1952.
Yeats, W. B. *Letters*, ed. by A. Wade. London. 1954.

Index

Index

WIDENER UNIVERSITY
WOLFGRAM
LIBRARY
CHESTER, PA.

DATE DUE